THE GOLDEN THREAD

THE GOLDEN THREAD

Mair Blethers from the Brig

Brigadier Frank Coutts

B&W PUBLISHING

First published 2006
by B&W Publishing Ltd
99 Giles Street, Edinburgh, EH6 6BZ

ISBN 13 978 1 903265 15 4
ISBN 10 1 903265 15 0

Typeset by RefineCatch Ltd, Bungay, Suffolk
Printed and bound by Creative Print and Design Group Ltd

Contents

Acknowledgements

I am extremely grateful to the following: my daughters, Fiona McCallum and Sheena Scott for editing, proof reading and encouragement; my son-in-law – author Alastair Scott – for assistance with photos and logos; my nephew Alastair Richmond for photographs; Brian Aldridge my computer advisor; Bill Hogg and other members of the Scottish Rugby Union staff; The Earl of Dalkeith, Millennium Commissioner; Mr George Ballinger, Chief Engineer and Patricia Rettie, British Waterways Scotland; Guthrie Hutton, author of books about the Scottish Canals; Norman Simpson, Seagull Trust for proof reading and encouragement; Marcel Adriaanse, former Pipe Major of the Inter Scaldis Pipe Band, Vlissingen, Holland; Mrs Frances Paxton and her sister Judith McLean, Hawick, for memorabilia of her father; Gideon Lumsden 4 KOSB Reunion and his successor Jim Coltman; Ian Martin, curator KOSB Museum, Berwick upon Tweed; Brigadier Colin Mattingley, Donald Fairgrieve, Major Alastair Hewat and Major William Turner, KOSB officers; and Alan Herriot, sculptor, for permission to print the photo of his statuette in the Scottish Room of the Overloon Netherlands War Museum. Long may they flourish.

Commendations for The Golden Thread

Here is another splendid offering from the remarkable Coutts family, who, between them, have contributed so much to Scottish – and British – life and write so entertainingly about their experiences.

Sir Max Hastings

I have read Frank's 'blethers' with great interest. Few can have had such a varied life, crowned with so much success. The chapters on the Scottish Regiments and Scottish Rugby are naturally close to my heart. The demise by stealth of our famous Regiments has been disgraceful, so much has been lost and nothing gained. One day we will be proved right. When I was President of the SRU Frank was my No 2 and our thinking through the professional shambles was always the same. The lead for improvement must come through the clubs, who are the real strengths of Scottish Rugby. I wish *The Golden Thread* every success and I'm delighted to give it my support.

Lord Hector Monro of Langholm

After *One Blue Bonnet* in 1991, it has been well worth the wait for Brigadier Frank Coutts's latest offering. If he had not already found a sub-title for *The Golden Thread*, he could have called it *Refreshingly Frank*! For that describes these uninhibited outpourings of a brave soldier, now relieved of military decorum and having reached an age when he can say what he really thinks – and damn the consequences!

To great effect, Frank Coutts lashes out at Defence Minister Geoffrey Hoon and his coterie of colonels for what they have done to the Scottish regiments. He is no less frank with the inadequacies of the Kirk, in which his own father was a memorable minister.

As a Scottish rugby internationalist, he has plenty to say about the state of the game today. And, if he had none of these controversies to hold our attention, the remarkable story of the Coutts family itself would have been worth the money.

On top of all that, there's the wisdom of a great human being, some surprising opinions – and humour that rounds off the delightful read.

Jack Webster

A distinguished son of the manse and soldier, Brigadier Frank Coutts, in his latest book, expresses his views with clarity and conviction as he reflects on his long and varied life. 'Service not Self', the motto of the Royal British Legion Scotland, of which he was General Secretary on retirement from the Army, sums up his immense contribution to Scotland and the UK in the many areas of his interest and commitment. The reader may or may not agree with his views and opinions but will certainly find them stimulating. I commend *The Golden Thread* which makes a distinctive contribution to many issues which exercise our concern.

The Very Reverend Dr James Harkness
KCVO CB OBE MA DD

Preface

WHY 'GOLDEN THREAD'?

When the Right Honourable Geoffrey Hoon MP, Minister of Defence, rose in the House of Commons to disband the six remaining Scottish Regiments – without a tremor in his voice – he said: 'There will be no change. *The Golden Thread of Tradition will run through the new Regiment, the Royal Regiment of Scotland.*' I'd like to meet the idiot civil servant who drafted these words. They are absolute balderdash. No change? In the case of the King's Own Scottish Borderers, who are to be merged with the Royal Scots, it is not a case of 'no change', for everything goes; there is nothing to change, the Regiment disappears – 316 years of history, thirty-one battle honours, the Freedom of Edinburgh and Berwick-upon-Tweed (in England) and sixteen burghs across the Borderland, our beloved cap badge, the uniform – especially the Leslie tartan trews (to be replaced by the totally unsuitable Government tartan kilt, alien to Borderers). A regiment is a family; in the case of the KOSB the family will be wiped out on 1 August 2006, the anniversary of their most treasured battle honour, that of Minden in 1759.

After Mr Hoon has been justifiably pilloried in Chapter 1, I'd like to think that the Golden Thread runs through the rest of the book. It hasn't appeared so far in the devolved Parliament, but it is very much in evidence at Murrayfield, in the eighty-three members of the Coutts-Fleming clan, in the Church of Scotland (despite its many detractors), in the world of piping, which has never been better worldwide, in charities like the Seagull Trust, which provides free canal cruising in

Scotland for disabled people, and in the countless number of people I have met during my life who are so worthy of admiration.

Above all, I have been so fortunate to have had a Golden Thread running through my own life – a happy home, a good school, a profession I enjoyed, a wonderful wife for fifty-six years and a successful and happy family.

Truly, I believe, A Life Fulfilled.

Frank Coutts

Edinburgh

Easter 2006

For Morag
who followed the flag for fifty-six years

The cap badge of the new Royal Regiment of Scotland
(photo courtesy of Commander of 52nd Lowland Brigade)

Chapter 1

THE ARMY IN SCOTLAND

They Got It Wrong

Thank goodness I can start this book by writing about something I really know about.

Of the forty-nine years I spent in the uniform of a Scottish Regiment – Highland Light Infantry cap badge for eight years at school, two years in the London Scottish in the ranks and thirty-nine in the King's Own Scottish Borderers – no fewer than thirty-one were spent in Scotland. Far too many, of course. I did manage two tours in the Far East, one in Denmark, two in Germany and occasional duties in Gibraltar, Cyprus, Aden and the Gulf. I was always asking the Military Secretary's Branch in the War Office (Ministry of Defence) to let me go abroad. The best they could do was Barnard Castle in Durham, Plymouth in Devon and Oswestry in Shropshire! The reasons for some of my failures I spelled out in detail in *One Blue Bonnet*. One interesting posting after another crashed – Baghdad, Trieste, Rheindalen, Malta GC. No real complaints from me, however. I always believed in 'Dae as ye're telt', even if it meant spending too little time overseas.

Looking back over the past fifty years, the most interesting development in the Army in Scotland has been the gradual takeover by the Highland Regiments from the Lowland, who looked on the Highland Regiments for a century rather as rebels who were 'agin the Government' – they were, in Trevor Royle's deliciously chosen words, 'bare-arsed bandits'. There are many reasons for their takeover bid. The 51st (Highland) Division and the London Scottish, proudly affiliated to the

Gordons, made a great name for themselves in the First World War. They must, even then, have had a good PR machine. In the Second World War the PR machine worked flat out, with tree trunks from El Alamein to Berlin festooned with the Highland Division logo – which gained them the nickname of 'the Highland Decorators'. One rarely heard of the equally competent 52nd Lowland Division, which was mainly officered by douce Edinburgh and Glasgow lawyers who didn't believe in self-publicity. Then in June 1940 came the tragedy of St Valery when the Highland Division was decimated. But the Lowland Division was also chased out of France while taking part in the ludicrous Second British Expeditionary Force, a gallant gesture by Churchill to bolster up the retreating French army. Prepared to take on the might of the German army, the 52nd were nevertheless ordered to withdraw to Cherbourg, where they had to ditch most of their heavy equipment in the harbour.

Despite all this, the Government, which really meant Winston Churchill, chose to re-form the Highland Division and send them out to the Middle East while the 52nd Division, raring to go and fully manned, were sidelined to spend three years in the Highlands, pretending they were going to attack Norway which, of course, was never going to happen. Eventually, they were properly employed in Holland and Germany for the last nine months of the war and acquitted themselves well. For more detail on this you can read Peter White's excellent book *With the Jocks*.

The most important reason for the ascendancy of the Highland Regiments was that of personalities. The Highland Regiments produced a string of outstanding generals, so many that it is easy to roll them off the tongue – Archie Wavell, General 'Tartan Tam' Wimberley, 'Tiny' Barber, Peter Hunt, Brigadier Bernard Fergusson, the MacMillans – father and son – Gordon and John, Derek Lang, Geordie Gordon Lennox – you could go on and on. Whereas, by comparison, the Lowlands to this day have provided pygmies, relatively speaking, for the most part. The General Officer Commanding the 52nd Division during the war was the genial and popular 'Sir Hak' – we knighted him long before he officially got his 'K'. Major General Edmund Hakewill-Smith of the Royal Scots Fusiliers did a good job training a so-called Mountain Division for three frustrating years. They learned to ski on heather during the exceptionally mild winters and he constantly badgered the top brass for some real action – which I suspect made him pretty unpopular in Whitehall. Only George Collingwood, 'the Wicked Uncle', and our own KOSB Willow Turner were men of stature who could influence the increasingly important Council of Colonels, the very Council that has taken responsibility for the scandalous Hoon proposals of 2005.

I'll never forget the talent assembled in the Ladies' Room at Edinburgh Castle in 1968 when the Council met to decide which two Regiments should be disbanded under the Labour Government's proposals, led by Secretary of State Denis Healey. Listed in *One Blue Bonnet*, they are well worth repeating: Major General Bill Campbell, the Royal Scots, the Royal Regiment; Lieutenant General Henry Leask, the Royal Highland Fusiliers; our own Lieutenant General Willow Turner; Major General Henry Alexander, the Cameronians, Scottish Rifles (a difficult customer, especially over horse-flesh); Brigadier Bernard Fergusson, resentful that his tour as Colonel had come so late (but if you want to be Governor General of New Zealand like your father you can't have it both ways!); General Peter Hunt of the Queen's Own Highlanders (Her Majesty the Queen offered him a Field Marshal's baton but he declined, saying that he could not possibly accept as he had spent his entire tour disbanding half of her Army – what a gentleman!); General Geordie Gordon Lennox, Gordon Highlanders (who wasn't really a Gordon but a Grenadier

3

Guardsman), a real fighter with a wife to match – she didn't half shake up the Works Department at Gogarbank House!

To digress for a moment, they were very kind to us at Gordon Castle in Fochabers. After General Gordon Lennox retired I had the difficult task, set for me as a member of the Scottish Sports Council, of putting the Council's view to him in the notorious and never-ending canoes versus fishermen confrontation on the River Spey. He wouldn't give in, but respected my argument.

Last on the Council, but certainly not least, was the jovial, irrepressible 'Black & White' – half of his moustache was white and the other half black – Freddie Graham of the Argyll and Sutherland Highlanders. He was elected Chairman against the wishes of the General Officer Commanding-in-Chief Sir Derek Lang, who felt strongly – and I with him – that the GOC and the Chairman of the Council should be the same person.

The Council only took ten minutes – I was Secretary and the minutes are on record – to decide that the principle of 'last in, first out' should apply and so the Cameronians went from the Lowland Brigade and the Argylls had to go from the Highland Brigade. The Cameronians went – and a sad day it was – but, as we'll see, the Argylls wouldn't go.

General Freddie and his wife Phyll were very generous hosts at their house at Thornhill near Stirling and I remember one eventful dinner there when my staff car driver, Corporal Archie Douglas, arrived at the table holding the gear lever of his vehicle forlornly in his hand. Archie wasn't going anywhere that evening and our slight transportation difficulty was only overcome by squeezing into Tommy and Sheana Lamb's car. Tommy was the Highland Brigade's colonel. After dinner, regardless of the company, the highlight of the evening was General Freddie telling his favourite story about 'the cleg'. As with most stories, it was as much in the telling, but it goes like this.

A pompous Englishman was shooting in the Highlands when he was bitten on the nose by a cleg. He killed it dead with his hand and held it out to McTavish the ghillie. 'What is this?' he asked.

The ghillie replied, 'That's a cleg, sir. A wee black beastie that flees roon a coo's erse.'

Horrified, the Englishman replied, 'McTavish, you're not implying anything, are you?'

'Well, sir, all I can say is the cleg's awfie hard tae bamboozle!'

Another of the wartime generals who deserves, and never got, a mention is General 'Bulgy' Thorne, the General Officer Commanding-in-Chief of Scottish Command during the war. He used to visit us regularly, the cause of much spit and polish, in his lovely old Rolls Royce, nicknamed 'the Old Grey Mare', which was presented to him by a grateful Morningside lady. We thought him just an old fuddy-duddy, surrounded by many staff-wallahs in First World War leather leggings and the odd Polish General. In fact we only discovered after the war that he was the author of the brilliant operation which persuaded the Germans, by many secret means, that we were actually a Corps of three Divisions in Scotland, thus convincing the Boche that we really meant to invade Norway and forcing them to tie up thousands of troops who would otherwise have been in Normandy. He was an unsung hero of the Second World War.

The Old Grey Mare lasted long enough to take General Gordon MacMillan and myself round most of the Territorial Army Association meetings in Scotland between 1950 and 1952 until the Royal Electrical and Mechanical Engineers finally declared it BLR (beyond local repair). I hope it is preserved in some museum or other.

The different disbandments and amalgamations imposed by successive post-war Governments caused pain and grief to regimental families. I can't speak for the amalgamation of the Seaforth and Camerons but, knowing the fierce loyalties on both sides, where even villages on Speyside were loyal to different regiments, it must have been very difficult. The resultant Battalion, the Queen's Own Highlanders, was a fine body of men, whom I met in Selarang Barracks in Singapore under the fierce Charlie McHardy, who later became the Queen's factor at Balmoral. When I asked a corporal if the food was good he replied in a strong Highland twang, 'Same boring old seven choices, Sir.' Army catering has come a long way since I ate my first meal, which was kippers, before 'eating irons' (knife, fork and spoon) had been issued.

The further amalgamation with the Gordons was a tragedy for the Aberdeenshire and Buchan Regiment. They had traditionally relied on the farming loons ('teuchters') to fill their ranks but the oil boom defeated them completely, offering any number of well-paid jobs, and they couldn't recruit except by poaching on Black Watch territory in Dundee – much to the annoyance of Bernard Fergusson, the Colonel of the Black Watch.

The Lowland amalgamations were also extremely difficult. The first was the merger of the Royal Scots Fusiliers in Ayrshire, a proud county Regiment, the 21st of Foot, dating from 1689 and the Highland Light Infantry, which, as the name implies, was a Regiment formed by the many Highland families who settled in Glasgow after the Clearances. The regiments were very different in character, as were the Colonels, General Hakewill-Smith for the Fusil-Jocks and General Roy Urquhart (Highland Light Infantry) who had commanded the Airborne Division so gallantly at Arnhem. They simply couldn't agree on anything and a stalemate arose which was not helped by the MOD pressing them. They finally agreed that both should resign and two White Knights arrived in the shape of Brigadier Ian Buchanan-Dunlop for the Royal Scots Fusiliers – who had been twice my boss at different times, and, after retiral, our next-door neighbour in Colinton – and General Ronald Bramall-Davies for the Highland Light Infantry. They were just the sane voices that were required and the Royal Highland Fusiliers are now a well-established Regiment in the Scottish Division.

As both the Highland and Lowland experiences through the years have demonstrated, amalgamation is always a painful and unpleasant process but it is also a necessary evil.

So what of 'Hoonery' and why has it gone so badly wrong? The Hoonery I'm referring to is, of course, the 2005–06 reorganisation of the Scottish Regiments proposed by the Right Honourable Geoffrey Hoon MP, with the apparent agreement of the Council of Scottish Colonels under the Chairmanship of Lieutenant General Sir Alastair Irwin who was at that time the Colonel of the Black Watch and Adjutant General. This was an unacceptable combination and he should have done the honourable thing and resigned – in the Services, when things go wrong, it is always the 'top man' who gets the chop or resigns. You can just see the Army Board rubbing their hands with glee and saying, 'Now's the time to fix these bloody Jocks once and for all.' We'll see shortly why the actions of Hoon and Irwin are so roundly condemned by so many, but was there any logic behind their proposals?

The Government of the day is, of course, perfectly entitled to make sweeping changes in our defence as and when the international situation demands. It does seem that a peace dividend may be forthcoming in Northern Ireland, but to disband four infantry Battalions when our commitments abroad are actually increasing is Government stupidity of a very high order. Iraq is insoluble, things in Afghanistan are going from bad to worse – the Dutch won't go unless they are 'Protected' – there are other commitments elsewhere and new ones keep cropping up. We need infantry boots on the ground, not technology or nuclear submarines which cost the earth. It took even me by surprise when I read a statement in the House of Lords just before Christmas 2005 that we now have British troops stationed in no fewer than fifteen different foreign locations – Iraq, Bosnia, Kosovo, Afghanistan, Qatar, Bahrain, the South Atlantic, Diego Garcia, Cyprus, Gibraltar, the Congo, Georgia, Iberia, Sierra Leone, and the Sudan.

What a time to unfold a major reorganisation of the British Infantry! It is becoming increasingly clear that the Labour Government headed by Mr Blair has taken the view that the Armed Forces are an expensive luxury and they must be kept constantly at work. When he visits them he calls them 'our boys' but he has no compunction about increasing their overstretch while at the same time cutting numbers. It has also emerged that the Government's defence strategy, pompously named *Delivering Security in a Changing World*, was nothing to do with the changing face of conflict but solely an exercise prompted by the Chancellor of the Exchequer. Because of the appalling waste in the Procurement Department costing billions of pounds, the only way to square the defence budget was to make more troop cuts.

The scandalous waste in the procurement of defence equipment is worth a book on its own. Briefly, we have helicopters that can't fly above 500 feet and are no use in Afghanistan, the Eurofighter has already cost over £9 billion and is only one-third through its programme, BAE-built planes have been fitted with the wrong wings and, worst of all, the 'soldier's best friend', his rifle, is the despised SA80, which has been a disaster from the start.

All this is managed by forty-one Admirals in a Navy with only forty ships, by forty Air Marshals in an RAF with only thirty-six squadrons of aeroplanes, and in an Army which has only two operational Divisions, 180 Brigadiers (I blush), and sixty Generals. Surely something wrong there.

Reverting to reality and the crucifixion of the Scottish Regiments, the cancellation of the Arms Plot and the permanent location of Battalions in the same place for ever and ever amen, will no doubt delight the soldiers' wives and families. The continuity of education for the kids will certainly be a benefit – although it didn't do ours any harm to learn the four-letter words at an early stage in various Army schools at home and abroad. In fact, soldiers will still have to move to different locations very often, depending on Extra-Regimental Employments, promotion and so on, and those who are foolish enough to buy houses near what they think is a permanent location will undoubtedly find themselves with a millstone round their necks. So it's perhaps not as rosy a picture as some might suggest.

Put at its simplest, they had absolutely no right to disband Regiments whose spirit has helped Great Britain to win every conflict in which it has been involved for over 300 years. *They got it wrong*. When Regiments were totally independent, answering direct to the War Office and MOD, they were shocked when they were ordered to go into two Brigades, Lowland and Highland. They hated it, especially the odious cap badge that went with it – in the case of the Lowland, a sort of bus driver's safe-driving award (with apologies to Lothian Regional Transport). The change came when we were in Malaya and Regiments were invited to design the new badge incorporating details of each of the (then) five Lowland Regiments. Hugh Gillies, our Second-in-Command, had the greatest fun designing spoof badges, one of which incorporated the Highland Light Infantry's Assaye Battle Honour of an elephant evacuating its bowels over the walls of Edinburgh Castle.

The difference between then and now is that each Regiment was *in* one of the two Brigades, for example the King's Own Scottish Borderers was in the Lowland Brigade. Ten years later the Scottish Division was formed, ending the traditional enmity between Lowland and Highland. I had the privilege of forming it and it was nae bother. Regiments were still referred to as the Such-and-Such *in* the Scottish Division. This time the men in grey suits have put it the other way round. We are now to be the Royal Regiment of Scotland (brackets, Such-and-Such a Regiment). A totally unnecessary and unwarranted change.

Incidentally, talking of cap badges, the proposed new cap badge for the unwanted Royal Regiment of Scotland is no advance on the perfectly good badge of the Scottish Division, which the Lord Lyon King of Arms described as 'heraldically impeccable'. Enough said.

So how did it all come about? It's clear to many that the Scottish Council of Colonels was bullied by the Chief of the General Staff and his ally, General Irwin of the Black Watch. It was not a unanimous decision and with a wee bit more smeddum the Council could easily have stood up to the MOD. I was Secretary of the Council for two years and a full member for ten – twice as long as any serving or retired Colonel, apart from Garry Barnett of the Black Watch, who like me is an active opponent of the present 'reorganisation'. Our decisions were always unanimous. This decision was *not* unanimous. The Colonel of the King's Own Scottish Borderers was on duty in Afghanistan and he was represented by Brigadier Andrew Jackson, a third-generation Borderer. His grandfather recruited me and I recruited him. He voted against the Hoon proposals as the Royal Scots and the Royal Highland Fusiliers should have done, but the Council was in thrall to the Highlanders, who meekly followed their leader and carried the motion 5–1. *And the people of Scotland were never consulted* although they have made their views pretty clear in the press during 2005. A petition signed by 150,000 Scots was delivered to Number 10 Downing Street on St Andrew's Day 2005: a clear message that the people of Scotland demand to have *their* Regiments reinstated.

If one Regiment had to go, it should not have been the KOSB but the Argylls, who were ordered to disband by Denis

Healey and their own Colonel in 1968 but wriggled out of it thanks to the antics of Colonel Colin 'Mad Mitch' Mitchell in Aden and the jovial chicanery of General Freddie Graham. There is an imbalance of Regiments between Highland and Lowland. It is also a slap in the face for the (awful) Scottish Parliament, for the capital city of Edinburgh, which has granted its Freedom to two Lowland Regiments, for the Borders, and for the commercial centre of Glasgow with its neighbouring counties of Lanarkshire and Ayrshire, which provide most of the recruits for the Army in Scotland anyway.

The final indignity is forcing the Lowlanders, and particularly Borderers, to wear the kilt. Imagine a chap in Newcastleton ('Copshawhame') being asked to wear the kilt! The kilt is the dress which was worn (if at all) by the Highland Companies which formed the basis to the highly successful Highland Regiments. Their ancestors – read *The Steel Bonnets* by George MacDonald Fraser – fought against the English for generations. And later ancestors fought against the Highland rebels at Killiecrankie and Culloden. They should not be compelled to wear the garb of Old Gaul. And the Government tartan! An added insult. It's so dark it's fit for a funeral.

Time to end this tirade. I've probably lost half of my friends but, oh, it was good getting it off my chest!

Well, maybe not quite. Not unnaturally some of the 'Old and Bold' in the KOSB decided that we will not put up with this. After all, this is a democratic country and protests agin the Government are two-a-penny. So the Edinburgh Branch of the KOSB Association, myself included, formed a 'Save the KOSB' committee to oppose the disbandment of Scottish Regiments and the merger with the Royal Scots. We worked within the policies of the Save Our Scottish Regiments campaign organised by Jeff Duncan and supported mainly by the Black Watch and the KOSB, whose efforts were energetically put together by the indomitable Brigadier Allan Alstead, an outstanding former

Commanding Officer of the 1st Battalion and deeply involved in many other causes. The *modus operandi* was to have a go at MPs, the media, every possible outlet for informing the Scottish public of the grave damage which was being done to our Scottish Regiments.

The campaign has had only a limited effect on the Scottish public who, in peacetime, are much more interested in fitba'. Serving officers and soldiers had of course to follow the party line and support the reforms, while obviously disagreeing with them. This has caused a rift between those who wish the proposals to go through, which they will, and those of us who, from the beginning, felt they were wrong, wrong, wrong. And said so. As a result the 'military' in Scotland has been split down the middle, our phones have been tapped, and long-cherished friendships have been put at risk.

The strain which this put on Regimental loyalty is very severe. We had no argument with the Royal Scots – I served with them in the same Brigade for five years in war and two in peacetime. The principal object of the Save Our Scottish Regiments campaign was to try to convince the Government that the world situation simply did not permit four Battalions of Infantry to be struck off at this dangerous time and that the disbandment by name of all the Scottish Regiments was a ridiculous over-reaction in the cause of 'modernisation'.

The Save the KOSB campaign also claimed that the merger with the Royal Scots was illegal under Scots law. The KOSB was raised in Edinburgh in March 1689 – eighteen years before the Act of Union in 1707 – by a Scottish Act of Parliament which specified that Leven's Regiment, the 25th of Foot, 'could not be interfered with save by the passage of a further law'.

The Ministry of Defence lawyers have clearly been in a total muddle. The case has been to court before a magistrate who deemed the court unable to hear the case. It now goes to the

Court of Session before a Sheriff Principal. Whatever the outcome, the Borderers have won the moral high ground by showing that the Regiment will never give in but will fight to the end.

Eventually, it was decided that the cost of taking this judgement to the High Court was too high and would be contrary to the spirit which had to activate the Royals and the KOSB. The cap badge was adopted on 28 March 2006 and the 'merger' takes place almost four months later on 1 August, a date dear to the heart of all King's Own Scottish Borderers – Minden Day.

After long and distinguished service, I wish Generals Jackson and Irwin a happy retirement. I'm afraid that they will suffer from nightmares from time to time when they come to realise the damage they have done to the British Infantry. But I don't suppose the Rt Hon. Geoffrey Hoon MP will lose much sleep – he was just the stooge who had to read out the ill-considered policy put in his hands.

Now that I have had my say and the deed is done, I naturally wish the new Regiment every possible success. I am delighted to hear that recruiting is going well. It does not surprise me because the Director of Army Recruiting is an officer in the King's Own Scottish Borderers.

The expensive new parliament building at Holyrood (photo courtesy of Michael Wolchover)

Chapter 2

DEVOLUTION

I'm Sure They Got It Wrong

In my opinion, devolution and the Scottish Parliament are a disaster and should never have been allowed to happen. I must say I was staggered at the seventy-plus per cent of Scots who voted for it. I never met anyone who voted Yes–Yes. I must move among the wrong kind of people! My brother Ben was one who voted Yes. He said that the administration of agriculture could never be so bad as it was in London – but he soon changed his mind when he saw the sort of people who would be in charge in Edinburgh. Politically, he was a maverick. He stood for Parliament as a Liberal Democrat and he gave Nicky Fairbairn a good run for his money in Perth and Kinross, but his lifestyle was Tory to the core and I think in the end he was so angry with Jim Wallace for cosying up with Labour that he would have voted Conservative.

I'm as Scots as they come. Born just off the Great Western Road in Glasgow, the fourth son of a Church of Scotland minister, I went to school in Glasgow, served most of my life in Scottish Regiments, married a fellow Glaswegian who was born just round the corner from me, played rugby for Scotland and played the bagpipes to quite a high standard. But I am British (Scots), not the other way round. The whole performance of devolution reminded me so much of the 1945 election when the returned ex-servicemen and women gave Winston Churchill the boot, after he'd saved the country from becoming a satellite of Hitler's Germany. The election result was declared to be the first and only Battle Honour of the Royal

Army Education Corps, who revelled in their role of preaching socialism to the wartime sailors, soldiers and airmen. I know; I heard 'em. And before commanding a Junior Soldiers' Battalion I went to their Headquarters at Eltham Palace and was indoctrinated about political correctness. Shame. They were such nice people.

It all seems such a pity to me. Scotland has a wonderful record, through its ancient and splendid universities, of providing a disproportionately high number of administrators of those territories which we admired so much in our school atlases. 'That's coloured red so it must be British,' we would purr. And the teachers, many of whom were educated in England, would not disagree. Then, after Churchill, that fine wartime hero President Roosevelt, who held the world's purse strings, upset the applecart. He had a bitter and lasting hatred for colonialism as a consequence, I suppose, of the history of his own country under the Brits and spared no thought for the millions of Africans and others who would be left leaderless. He bullied Churchill – or rather 'Wind of Change' Macmillan – into handing over our reasonably stable territories to a bunch of crackpots like Idi Amin. And we have seen the result – now landed on George W. Bush's plate – with the 2005 G8 summit meeting (at Gleneagles of all ridiculous places) being asked to provide aid for the starving millions of Africa. They never starved – even during wartime – when the Brits were administering their countries. Ironically, America's role in world affairs now makes her the biggest colonial power in the twentieth and twenty-first century.

Our predominance in colonial affairs was one of the causes of the drive for independence. Scotland became inward-looking instead of leading the way in world administrators. Then there was the underlying Anglophobia, mostly confined to the football field, but always there – sometimes justified when the English don't bother to come north and see what a wonderful country it is, or when the BBC don't teach their announcers how to pronounce Scottish names like *For*far and Lo*ch* Lomond. Their tongues just seem incapable of pronouncing the *ch* sound. It remains an absolute scandal that the England–Scotland Football International cannot be played because the last time it happened the Scottish drunken hooligans invaded the pitch at Wembley and tore down the goalposts. There are many young people, perhaps some of them reading this, who would not believe that such a thing could happen. Perish the day that it should happen at Murrayfield!

Always lurking there is the Scottish National Party. They are a pretty disorganised rabble now but, if and when Alex Salmond decides to come back from Westminster, he could provide a real threat to the shaky Lab–Lib coalition. He is among the top speakers in the House of Commons and, if he could pick political allies as well as he picks racehorses, we could be facing a fate worse than devolution. Colin Campbell, their former defence spokesman, writing from the fortress of Benbecula, is always good for a giggle. He would raise again the nine Scottish Regiments at once. Goodness knows what they would all do if they were not in the British Army. Where would they live? And what would it cost?

Here's the nub of it. Scotland's First Minister should not be monkeying about making foreign visits to Africa or New York in a loin cloth. Our economy is already beginning to suffer under the legally empowered Scottish Executive. We should be an integral part of a strong Great Britain, closely allied to the USA and the Commonwealth, with the minimum allegiance to Europe, repealing everything back to the European Economic Community, no more. The diktats from the falsely titled European Union fanned by the twice-discredited Mr Mandelson pour out daily.

And what sort of legislation has the so-called Scottish Parliament introduced? Every oppressive option in the book. They've banned fox-hunting and smoking and they're busy thinking up more. Grouse shooting will probably be next, then fishing. After that – sexual intercourse? Of course they want 'more powers' and fifty per cent of the Scottish people seem to agree. One MSP at least has had the honesty to admit that they should be part-time and I'd suggest the expenses should be reduced proportionately. Headlines like 'Holyrood wages bill soars' are quite a common sight and the press have not helped. Most are pro-devolution, warts and all. I used to read *The Scotsman*'s agricultural correspondent – but not now. The language about the farming community who enjoy fox-hunting as a pastime is positively vitriolic and puerile. The Scottish Executive should be doing something about people in Glasgow who tear each other to bits every Saturday night, not hounds and foxes.

Then there are the people! With the lure of huge salaries, expenses and pensions, the Parliament has produced a string of mediocrities.

John Smith might have made a go of it but Donald Dewar seemed to me to be a strange character. I've no right to say that because I did not know him, but there's no doubt he was dedicated to the cause of devolution and was determined to see it through, no matter the cost. I say 'strange' because he seems to have had a strange relationship with money. It was well known that when he was Secretary of State he purposely lunched every day in the canteen rather than in the dining room reserved for senior members of the administration. At the end of his meal he would – with a flourish aimed at his audience – take a piece of bread, wipe his plate clean and swallow the bread. And yet he left a considerable sum of money in his will – unusual behaviour, I'd say. As a fellow Glasgow Academical I should have been bursting with pride at his achievements. His bust, without spectacles, has, I believe, been placed honourably in the Cargill Hall at his old school.

No one can possibly excuse the enormous waste of public money on the new Scottish Parliament building which is Donald

Dewar's legacy. So much has been written that I will not comment on the abominable scandal of it all, except to say that I toured it the other day and became angrier and angrier at the enormous pomposity of it all. Everyone had told me how impressive the debating chamber is. My reaction was to turn to my daughter and say, 'It wouldn't surprise me if one o' yon beams cam' doon one day and hit an MSP on the heid.'

To have the abysmal cheek of placing the new parliament building right beside Her Majesty's principal residence in Scotland, the Palace of Holyroodhouse, was sheer presumption, especially when there was an alternative ready to hand. The Royal High School building was just right for a small devolved body to run purely Scottish affairs. It is a fine chamber – I have attended conferences there – and it could have been made a splendid location for what Tony Blair rightly called 'just a sort of County Council'. The press complained that there were inadequate facilities for them. Who the hell do they think they are? I would have put them in Nissen huts on Calton Hill.

The only change we needed from the status quo was a well-attended meeting of the Scottish Grand Committee with devolved powers, meeting every Friday, attendance obligatory. It was always poorly attended by Scottish MPs, shame on them, and they got their comeuppance. I am surrounded in my humble abode by retired civil servants from the old Scottish Office and they all say it worked perfectly well. There was simply no need for change. *They got it wrong.*

A lot of my predictions have come true over the years and maybe my grandchildren will live to see the Scottish parliament building turned into another attraction (as if there weren't enough already) on the Royal Mile and the Royal High building restored to its true glory.

And what of the future? That dangerous and able man, Alex Salmond MP, has come clean with the question he wants the Scottish National Party to put to the Scottish people on independence – although not till 2011, praise be. The question which would be put once the SNP gained a majority in the Scottish Parliament would be: 'Should the Scottish Parliament negotiate a new settlement with the British Government so that Scotland becomes a sovereign and independent State?' A declaration of sovereignty would then be drawn up by the Scottish Parliament. Mr Salmond, presenting a document entitled *Raising the Standard*, forecast that the elections in May 2011 would be 'within an independent nation'. He stressed that many of the subjects reserved to Westminster such as immigration (he called it 'asylum-seekers'), state pensions and nuclear power would be decided by Holyrood.

Salmond didn't mention defence but perhaps he should have, because he was the only Westminster MP who stood up for the Scottish Regiments when they were cruelly disbanded by the Labour Government in 2005/6. On that issue I suppose you could say that he was toadying up to the many voters in his Buchan constituency who would be fervent supporters of the Gordon Highlanders, now a part of *the Highlanders* or, sorry, the 4th Battalion of the Royal Regiment of Scotland. At least he had the guts to stand outside Parliament on St Andrew's Day 2005 and join the protesters delivering a petition to Number 10 Downing Street, voicing the, surely, unanimous demand of Scotland: 'Can we have our Regiments back please?'

But just how would the SNP deal with defence matters? The defence of Britain, including Scotland, is a matter for the British Government. There are vast tracts of Scotland owned by the Ministry of Defence in London, not to mention the nuclear submarine base at Faslane, and huge air bases, giving good employment opportunities, at Kinloss, Lossiemouth and Leuchars. The Army owns or leases considerable tracts of land for training in addition to several headquarters and Territorial and Cadet centres up and down the country. None of these facilities could be passed over to a Scottish 'Government'. The contribution of Scots personnel and expertise towards the defence of Great Britain has always been of a high order and much respected throughout the UK.

Shiver my timbers. As a former Scottish soldier, I'm used to refraining from politics but for the sake of my children and grandchildren I do hope that independence can be averted. Think hard about the consequences. Do you want to see the Scottish ambassador (*sic*) playing second fiddle to the British (English) ambassador in Paris, Berlin, Moscow, Washington? It beggars belief. Having insisted on all the Scottish Regiments wearing the kilt, no doubt the ambassadors would be required to wear the kilt all day long – even in hot climates.

If over seventy per cent of Scots voted for devolution at the referendum, would it be same under the SNP's referendum? I fervently pray that most people have learned their lesson. Life is no better under Jack McConnell than it was under Tony Blair.

But just how British are the Scots? Among the elderly population I would say we are very pro-British and very half-hearted (at best) about devolution. It all stems, I suppose, from royalty, for Her Majesty is Queen of Great Britain, Northern Ireland and most countries of the Commonwealth. At once I would say that those who lived through the Second World War would still be very 'pro' the Royal Family. They remember the stoicism of King George VI and Queen Elizabeth, a Scot from Glamis in Angus, when they opted to stay in London in order to be with their people. During the bombing raids they showed great sympathy when they visited the devastated streets and houses of the East End of London. Scots, too, are immensely proud, and particularly in Aberdeenshire and the North, of the royal family's love of Balmoral and Deeside and its couthy folk. It was heart-warming that Her Majesty decided to celebrate her eightieth birthday, in 2006, with a cruise to the Western Isles. The Princess Royal works tirelessly and is widely popular in Scotland.

Among younger people in Scotland I suspect that the attitude towards the Royal Family would be less friendly. With the continuing equalisation of society, most youngsters look on 'toffs' with disdain. They also point to some of the less attractive goings-on among the younger members of the Royal Family. For a monarchy that rules under the divine right of kings, it is sad to record that no fewer than three of the Queen's children have been divorced, including the heir apparent.

Despite that, there is still huge support for the Queen throughout Great Britain and Northern Ireland and the Commonwealth. And, one could add, the rest of the world, who admire the stability Great Britain has achieved over a large number of years. In a recent poll I read that the Queen had overtaken Elvis Presley to become 'the third most popular act of all time' (I don't like 'act' – HM does not act; everything she does is genuine). Anyway, I do believe that the majority of people in Britain agree with the necessity to have a head of state who is surrounded by courtiers and has a dignified lifestyle. It is good to see that both of the royal princes have opted for training at Sandhurst. I just wish one of them would join a Scottish Regiment instead of becoming a 'Donkey Walloper' (the Jocks' name for a cavalryman).

Allied to the subject of royalty is that of the honours system, which increasingly attracts criticism – mostly from those who would dearly like to be included in the biannual list of the good and the great throughout Britain who have done honour to their profession and their country. Those who have never been to an investiture at Buckingham Palace or Holyroodhouse cannot imagine the thrill, not necessarily of the recipients, but principally of the next of kin who are lucky enough to receive tickets. It is a really heart-warming occasion. Other royal occasions, such as the recent tented lunch for ex-servicemen and women who served in the Second World War, or an invitation to dine at Buckingham Palace or Holyrood are occasions that people remember for a lifetime.

After the royalty question, the most important item must surely be the economy. Is it better or worse since devolution? Difficult to say from the outpourings of the financial pundits. I have some sympathy for those who say that it was Scotland's oil, though I doubt if we would have had the expertise to manage the vast industries involved in its production. A good deal of newspaper space, no doubt fanned by the nationalists, is now devoted to the possibility that full fiscal powers should be devolved from Whitehall to Holyrood – or rather to Leith, where a very large complex of offices houses the thousands of civil servants it now takes to run the 'County Council' of Scotland. There are apparently more people employed in public service than any other employment sector in Scotland.

Month by month the evidence emerges of the grave mistakes that have been made and the inefficiency that has accompanied devolution. The headlines, daily, are awesomely bad, but no one seems to care. The Scottish public voted for devolution and they are now beginning to realise what they let themselves in for.

For a start, the cost has been horrific. Due to inflation and public indifference, sums of money in millions of pounds cease to have a shock effect. Now it has been announced that devolution has cost in the first five years one *billion* pounds. Nearly half of that went on the outrageous and unnecessary Parliament building, added to which were administrative and property costs of £108 million. MSPs' salaries at £56 million are almost equalled by their noses-in-the-trough expenses of £54 million.

The Parliament in London doesn't seem to give a damn about the state of affairs in Scotland. This is surprising when one considers that a fair proportion of the senior ministers in the UK Parliament are Scots. Maybe they feel that the English are not up to running their own country? No wonder the Sassenachs are angry, because it is ludicrous that they have been denied their own regional assemblies and yet Scots MPs in Westminster are permitted to vote on matters affecting England, Wales and Northern Ireland only – a crazy state of affairs.

Astonishingly, the Conservative Party, who were one hundred per cent against devolution, are actually encouraging the adoption of full fiscal powers in Scotland. No wonder they languish in opposition. Perish the thought of droves of civil servants coming up from Whitehall to show the Scots how to tax themselves. No wonder our taxes and council taxes are so high. There is a large body of opinion in Whitehall which considers that Scotland is very well cared for by Westminster with its annual subsidy, called 'the Goschen formula' (who was Goschen?), first approved in 1888. It was replaced about twenty-five years ago by the Barnett formula.

The key factor is, of course, the economy, and it is very difficult to take a balanced view since devolution. Some commentators, mainly from the Confederation of British Industry (who surely have the best sources), indicate that the economy of Scotland is being strangled by the incompetence of the Scottish Parliament. I wouldn't go so far as the former Glasgow Academical, Professor Niall Ferguson who, pictured in front of the school's treasured War Memorial at Kelvinbridge, had the infernal cheek to say that Scotland's assets should be 'sold up and she should be liquidated'. After his professorship at Oxford when he produced some very worthwhile commentary on world affairs, I'm afraid the adulation of our American cousins has gone to his heid and he should be ashamed.

All this talk about devolved government implies that the Scottish Parliament and Executive have control over Scottish affairs in certain departments. Realistically of course, not even the United Kingdom Parliament has control over the affairs of Great Britain. It is now the so-called European Union which controls most of our legislation, and the individuals with powers are not Jack McConnell or even Tony Blair, but someone called Jose Manuel Barroso, the President of the European Commission, the former Portuguese Prime Minister. He was voted the person with most power in Britain by a BBC Radio 4 Poll, 'Who Runs Britain?', eclipsing Tony Blair, Gordon Brown and Rupert Murdoch, the press supremo. Radio 4 listeners certainly form a cross-section of the British public who really care about the British way of life and are justifiably concerned about the manner in which European laws are gradually eroding British life and customs. Increasingly one reads of retailers who are just not prepared to agree what size and shape sausages and other items are to be. How on earth can Mr Barroso know what kind of 'bangers' the English, Welsh, Irish and Scots prefer? And if you wish to judge the ludicrous size of the European Parliament, take a canal cruise round the European Parliament building in Strasbourg. It is so huge that it takes about half an hour to encircle it. Not just one Bridge Too Far but several. And against this European legislative onslaught stands Scotland's pompous wee Parliament. It's an unfair contest.

It would be interesting to know what Scotland's increasing number of immigrants think of the push-me-pull-you situation between Scotland and the British Parliament. Immigration is not a devolved subject and they all entered Britain – and welcome, with safeguards – seeking British nationality. There is absolutely no doubt that the Scottish economy has benefited from the arrival of a significant number of overseas immigrants. Commonwealth countries have provided numerous successful shopkeepers who are prepared to work very hard and for long hours – quite possibly breaking a few European regulations on the way! Would the SNP suggest that, once Scotland has gained independence, immigrants would be obliged to adopt Scottish nationality and not British?

I rest my case. Devolution has failed the people of Scotland in so many different ways *they got it wrong.*

International Football Match

OFFICIAL PROGRAMME

SCOTLAND

versus

WALES

At Murrayfield, Edinburgh
Saturday, 30th March 1946
KICK OFF 3 P.M.

Published with
Authority of the
SCOTTISH
RUGBY
UNION

PRICE
3D.

Programmes now cost a wee bit more!

Chapter 3

SCOTTISH RUGBY

Could They Have Got It Right?

Well, I can't actually say 'they got it wrong' because truthfully I don't know just how they could have got it right.

In cricketing terms, I'm batting on a pretty sticky wicket here. The Past Presidents of the Scottish Rugby Union, being merely *ex officio* members of the Union, by tradition do not speak or even vote at the Annual General Meeting and they have taken a vow of silence among themselves not to write to the press. They invariably give their full support to the current President. On the whole it's a good rule and it has been scrupulously followed over the years. It would have been very embarrassing if a PP had upped and spoken against the current President, say, whilst attending a District meeting as a club representative or a club dinner. On the other hand, it is somewhat frustrating to sit in the front row at the AGM like a stookie, unable to comment when the President of Auchtertoul RFC gets up and talks some utter tosh and needs putting in his place.

The AGM of 2005 abolished the old committee and I therefore feel freed from the vow of silence. I wonder what punishment the disciplinary committee would award a geriatric Past President for speaking out of turn?

Where did it all go wrong? The fundamental trouble was that the SRU was not ready for professional rugby. It came as a dreadful shock when Fred McLeod and Allan Hosie, our representatives on the International Rugby Board, came back from a meeting in Paris in 1995 saying: 'That's it. No argument. *The game is now open at every level.*' That meant professionalism.

Of the four Home Unions the SRU had always been not only amateur but fiercely so. The stories of its frugality, not to say meanness, are legion. We refused to play the French in 1933 because they were known to be paying players, and games with France only resumed after the Second World War, on 1 Jan 1947, when I was privileged to be present as a reserve and piper. Harry Simson, the stoical and charming Secretary, ran the Union from his lawyer's office at 10 Coates Crescent, expenses only. Everything had to be paid for – 'a penny for your morning newspaper, a penny for the weighing machine' at Murrayfield – and invitations to play in a trial or international arrived on a postcard with a penny stamp. When I was summoned to don the coveted blue jersey for a full international at Murrayfield I was stationed 'at the back o' beyond' on an anti-tank range in Jutland. The postcard informing me that I had been selected arrived three weeks after the match! I think the unkindest economy was that the players who had played before the war were told immediately after the war by Harry: 'Naw, naw, you don't get a new jersey – you had one in 1938/39' – Donnie Innes, Ian Henderson, Ralph Sampson, Bill Young and Copey Murdoch. To be fair to Harry, new rugby jerseys, like every other item of clothing, could only be bought with clothing coupons, which were not plentiful. They were pretty skimpy jobs anyway, with the proud blue thistle roughly sewn on to the left breast. Players' numbers, which had only recently been introduced by a reluctant committee a few years before, were stitched on and it didn't take much to pull them off in a Welsh tackle. Not the sort of thing you would proudly present to your grandson. But the caps, no doubt manufactured before the war, were magnificent, and mine has been duly presented to my grandson, who is a Scottish cricket international.

Gradually, the finances of the Union improved. They owned a superb property at Murrayfield and the international matches were well attended and brought in substantial monies, with expenditure limited to the match expenses and generous handouts to clubs and Districts. Herbert Waddell, he of the famous winning dropped goal in 1925, and his son had proved wise financial advisers, but everything changed when the word 'professionalism' emerged. It coincided with two things. First, the players were becoming restive; in a commercial world, they were beginning to say in the dressing rooms: 'Hey, this next ninety minutes of a performance put on entirely by us is going to net the Union about a million quid. Should we not be getting a little bit of that?' Second, a massive decision was taken to knock down most of Murrayfield and build a completely new stadium, the East Stand having been built quite recently, in the early 1980s. This decision was largely forced upon the Union by the demands of the Safety of Sports Grounds Act, which insisted on all-seated accommodation for grounds with a large capacity – and Murrayfield was three-quarters open terracing, prior to the 1980s. It was much loved by old stagers, but how lucky we were never to have a tragedy. At that famous Welsh match in 1975 when there were over 100,000 packed into the stadium, people were falling off the terracing and down the embankment. The old scoreboard had to go, but the clock on the south embankment, treasured as a rendezvous for many, and the War Memorial were relocated behind the East Stand.

The decision was announced very spectacularly on television. I was one of four Trustees and knew nothing of the decision until I saw Fred McLeod on the 'box' standing in the middle of the ground, proudly proclaiming that we were about to spend £41 million. It has proved a fine investment but at a heavy cost.

Then the arguments started about how professionalism was to be implemented. Suddenly the staff numbers at HQ escalated. From the single Harry Simson, who retired in 1951, the staff were modestly increased to John Law as Secretary and Douglas Cockburn, his assistant, with two girls in support. The ground staff were competently headed by Tom Sellars and Jim Thain, with three assistants. Now I believe there are about eighty persons employed at Murrayfield, supplemented on match days by a strong body of security men, who seem quite unable even to keep kids off the pitch at the end of game, despite repeated requests on the 'blower'. Similar requests not to whistle or jeer when opponents are preparing to kick at goal are equally ignored by today's young people, many there 'for free'.

The biggest argument of all was whether the clubs should become professional, as in England, or whether the District teams should be financed by the SRU and act as feeders for the national XV. The debate continued for about two years. Keith Robertson for Melrose and Scott Hastings for Watsonians spoke for the clubs, plus Brian Simmers for Glasgow Hawks, Finlay Calder for Stewart's Melville and the three Milne brothers – who were nicknamed the 'Three Milne Bears' – from Heriot's. They put forward a strong case but were outweighed by the gloomy rhetoric of Jim Telfer, the Director of Rugby. Since then the Districts have struggled to maintain a high place in the Celtic league, featuring Welsh and Irish Districts, Irish provinces, and Scottish Districts, despite the inclusion of several refugees from the Antipodes. The Districts tried to be fair to the clubs by playing mostly on a Friday evening and not on a Saturday afternoon. Only Edinburgh under Frank Hadden seemed to show some real promise of success. Sitting on a cold February evening at Meadowbank, where the pitch is even further away than at Murrayfield, is not an exciting prospect for oldies, though I'm told the social amenities are excellent and attracting a growing number of adherents. The alternative of playing at Murrayfield has little appeal; a crowd of 4,000 or 5,000 in the large stadium find it hard to raise an audible cheer. Other options are being considered. For me, a good old muddy tussle between Melrose and Hawick on a Saturday afternoon is more my cup of tea. The partial success of the Edinburgh team reminded me that, way back, when Frank Moffat was President of Watsonians, I had ill-advisedly proposed to their annual dinner that Edinburgh would never produce a team like, say, Northampton, till all the clubs gave up their best players for an all-Edinburgh XV. I was heartily booed. Now we have an Edinburgh team, but not necessarily composed of Edinburgh club members. The professional District clubs have come to stay – very much at the expense (literally) of the clubs, who are the lifeblood of the game.

The most distressing thing about the advent of professionalism is that, with very rare exceptions, it has not improved the performance of the national XV. 'Marketing' became more important than the game itself. The arrival of people like 'Fireworks Phil' Anderton no doubt pleased the screaming youngsters, but that and the awful tune blared out when Scotland scored had the Past Presidents' row growling: 'This is awful; it's not rugby, it's showbiz!' One group of people who did not approve of the fireworks were Bill Elwood and his groundsmen, who had to clear the rubbish from the gutters in a very high and dangerous position. Professional coaching from a highly paid overseas coach didn't seem to produce wins, the crowds slumped and the game in Scotland went into decline. At one Murrayfield Welsh match there were said to be more Welshmen in the ground than Scots. The players didn't seem to be enjoying themselves either. Far too much time has been spent on coaching set moves that don't come off and not enough scope given for individual brilliance. Most of all our teams lacked *pace*. Time and again scrum halves like Blair and Cusiter would make clean breaks of fifty metres or more and there was no one there screaming for a pass. That's inexcusable. Other than Chris Paterson we hadn't a single back in season 2004/5 who could outstrip the opposition. The team should spend more time at Meadowbank learning to run faster and less time practising rucks and mauls, which are so very dull.

For the most part Scotland's professional internationals have been 'gey dreich'. People don't mind losing but they like to see Scotland play with fire in their belly. The game is international but it can be argued that a man will play better for the land of his birth than a temporary resident earning his crust.

Now a national sporting hero, Andy Irvine, is in charge with a new team of executives. They appear to have been appointed more for their business expertise than their knowledge of rugby. We must all wish Andy and his team well. He is a fine ambassador for the game. Bill Hogg retired in 2005, a fine successor to Harry Simson and John Law. Not many people know that he is at Myreside every Saturday morning winter and summer, refereeing and umpiring. Now that the game is seven days a week, no weekends off for Bill. At the 2005 General Meeting the SRU President said of him: 'Characters are the very heartbeat of our game. How fortunate therefore we are in Scotland to be able to thank this great character. He has an encyclopaedic knowledge of and incredible passion for Scottish Rugby . . . [He is] the master of the minute, the bulwark of the bye-law and the custodian of the Constitution . . . Bill has served Scottish Rugby unselfishly with unstinting determination to do the best for the sport he loves.' Hear, hear!

There must be hope for the future. Our youth policies have been highly praised. We'll always be underdogs as far as numbers are concerned, although it must be said that Ireland. both in their national and district teams, seem able to produce more passion at Lansdowne Road than we do at Murrayfield.

We always said it would take ten years to acclimatise to professional rugby. That period has now elapsed and, as I write in 2005/6, it looks as though things are beginning to settle down and take shape, though there are still huge problems, mainly of finance.

After much argument and an agonisingly long appraisal, the Aussie coach departed and the successful Edinburgh coach,

Frank Hadden, was appointed. Straight away his team beat the Barbarians at Pittodrie and the team seemed to be enjoying themselves more. Come the Autumn Tests the improvement was visible, with narrow wins against Argentina and Samoa, two very hard teams to beat, composed as they are of players turning out for teams in the top range of professional rugby in France, New Zealand and elsewhere. Some pace was injected with the arrival of the Lamont brothers (accent on the first syllable please). We all knew the test would come against the All Blacks at the end of November 2005. This may have proved the turning point for a decade of disappointments. You can't fill the ground unless the Scottish team is really performing. The boys played magnificently and actually drew the second half 7–7 with some really rousing play. In the two previous games our backs often got within yards of the opponent's line but could never get the ball over it. I remember turning to my neighbour and saying: 'Why don't they try a grubber kick'? I must have been psychic for that was the way they scored against the All Blacks. Most importantly, it brought the crowd to its feet and that would assure better attendances in the Six Nations.

For the Kiwi game there was much media criticism of the cost of tickets and one has to agree that £60 for the best seats in the West Stand was pretty steep – and the remainder not much less. I was on duty in the North Stand at the World Cup Sevens and the stairs there are so steep that one almost has vertigo at the top. There is certainly a case for graduated ticket prices in accordance with visibility and accessibility.

We all knew that Bill McLaren was irreplaceable as the rugby commentator favoured by all nations. We are missing him terribly. The mistake most of them make is that they talk too much. Television is for watching the game, not listening to commentators' long-winded opinions. Jill Douglas is showing promise!

Incidentally, it is good to note that Bill McLaren's name appears in the Rugby International Hall of Fame. Although a fine player for Hawick in his day, until cruelly struck down by illness, he is the only non-capped player on the list of forty-nine names covering the last century. The other Scots are Gordon Brown, Gavin Hastings, Andy Irvine and Ian McGeechan. No sign of my schoolboy heroes, Jock Beattie of Hawick and Jock Allan of Melrose, Herbert Waddell of Glasgow Accies and Wilson Shaw of Glasgow High School. I suppose you could go on. It is indeed a rare honour.

Before we leave the International scene and move on to the Districts and the clubs – what happened to the International Trial? The last one was held so long ago that most readers won't remember it. It was usually played on the last Saturday of the year between the Blues (or Probables) and the Whites (Possibles). The spectators loved it – it gave them the chance to see the probable Scottish XV in action. The players certainly didn't love it! Especially if you were playing for the Probables and invited to join the Possibles at half-time. I should know – I 'done it'. The thrawn Scottish spectators invariably cheered for the underdogs, the Whites. Precious little good rugby was played – and the Possibles (or wrong) side usually won! I suppose that nowadays it would be almost impossible to arrange. With twenty-two players (at least) on each side there is no way that the professional clubs and Districts, especially in England and France, would give permission for their players to take part in a Scottish Trial. So that's another piece of Scottish Rugby history 'doon the dunny'.

The long-awaited improvement in the performance of the District and National XVs has cost a lot of money, some of which used to go to clubs, which, according to the Constitution, *are* the Scottish Rugby Union. They are now being disastrously neglected. Most are finding it difficult to make ends meet. Gate money is collapsing everywhere, and the cost of everything goes up.

An interesting feature of the programmes in the Autumn 2005 Tests was the inclusion, for the first time as far as I am aware, of the players' and replacements' schools (not clubs). The totals were revealing – ten had attended independent or Headmasters' Conference schools, whereas twelve had been educated at state or local authority schools, thus knocking on the head the old tag that rugby is played by toffee-nosed public-school snobs. Full marks to George Watson's, Preston Lodge and Berwickshire High, who each had two. It has been suggested that rugby-playing masters are more likely to be prepared to turn out (unpaid) on a Saturday morning than their football-playing colleagues. That will get me into deep trouble.

Perhaps this portrays too gloomy a picture of the 222 rugby clubs throughout Scotland. It is thriving in the Headmasters' Conference schools, despite the competition from a very wide range of sports nowadays. Dollar, Merchiston Castle and Edinburgh Academy are usually to the fore when it comes to the Schools Knock-out, sponsored by Bell, Lawrie. But local authority schools are playing some fine rugby too. Galashiels Academy knocked Dollar out of the 2005/6 Cup, not without a bit of aggro off the pitch. In the 2006 final between Stewart's Melville and Robert Gordon's College there were 6,200 spectators – 2,200 more than at any professional District game so far.

The BT League is still the premier achievement in Scottish Rugby. Although the routine club names are not so fully covered by the media due to the prominence of District and National matches, there is still a lot of good rugby being played around the country, in leagues well organised and monitored by the SRU. The supremacy of the Border clubs has waned somewhat in recent years, no doubt due to the creation of the Borders District team, the 'Border Reivers'. There was a fierce argument, of course, whether they would play at Netherdale, Galashiels or Mansfield, Hawick. Netherdale won, probably because of its accessibility from Edinburgh – and very well the

Gala club have fared in facilities as a result. It hasn't helped them much in the club championship, for they have swithered between struggling in the 1st Division and ruling the roost in the 2nd. It's sad to see a fine team like Kelso making heavy weather in the 2nd Division, but encouraging to see their near neighbours, Berwick (playing their rugby in England at Scremerston) having gradually squirmed their way up from a much lower division. Sad to see Langholm, who always get the biggest cheer at the Sevens when they occasionally score a try, really in the doldrums in one of the District leagues.

As a result of less pressure from the Border sides the city sides have crept up the ladders. Hawks in Glasgow are perhaps the hardest to beat. They started as an anticipated union between Hillhead and High Schools (H), Academicals (A), West of Scotland (W), Kelvinside (K) – and S presumably for the Simmer brothers who thought it all up! The team was designed as the Glasgow team of all the talents (see my Watsonians speech about an Edinburgh team of all the talents!). In the end most of the clubs went their own way, but the Hawks have flown high.

Dundee High School FP and Aberdeen Grammar School FP have come up in the world. That gives renewed hope for the fourth District, North/Midlands, to be created when money allows. There is now no mention of former clubs in the SRU programme! It may be that the majority of our professionals have no club loyalties at all, going straight from school or college to the rugby academy at Stirling.

Low down the leagues, it is sad to see founder members of the Union like Glasgow and Edinburgh Academicals teetering along amidst humble company – but they are enjoying their rugby and that's the important thing.

When finances allow, the SRU really must do more to help their clubs, which are the seedcorn, the grassroots of the game. Many clubs get into the red because the law imposes regulations which must be obeyed. Nature doesn't help. Poor Selkirk, and then Hawick, suffered unique flooding, not just once but twice. Clubs like Melrose which run successful seven-a-sides can probably cope, but smaller clubs have to rely only on subscriptions and levying the players for transport and so on. Rugby equipment alone now costs 'a ball'.

There is now one occasion in the year when the clubs really enjoy themselves and that is the final of the Knock-out competition at Murrayfield. The SRU committee voted against the Knock-out for years – and I take my share of blame for that opinion. But now it is a huge success, with families turning up in droves and enjoying a really festive day at Headquarters. It also gives dozens of club players the chance to play on the sacred turf of Murrayfield, in front of a substantial crowd, usually at a time of year when the weather is kind.

Talking about weather, the argument comes up from time to time about the amount of rugby which is lost during the period December–February, when grounds can frequently be unplayable, because of mud or frost. Summer rugby has been strongly advocated by the likes of Jim Telfer, whose opinions one listens to with respect. But there are too many snags. Summer is for cricket, the garden, bowls, holidays and so on, and anyway there is already a lot of rugby played during the summer months at home and abroad. It is not so long since the SRU bye-law stated: 'The season shall last from the 1st of September until the 30th of April.' Full stop. No argument. It was possible to ask permission to play a Sevens tournament in early May or late August, but permission was only granted with grunts of disapproval.

It is very heartening for old codgers from the Borders to see that much more attention is being given to the seven-a-side game than previously. When Edinburgh gave up their 'Charity' Sevens at Murrayfield, really the only notable Sevens outside of the Borders, there was actually a time when Edinburgh clubs declined to take part in the Borders Sevens because it interfered with the completion of their club programme. People have now come to realise, heavily prompted by those such as Lord Hector Monro of Langholm, that the running and tackling skills required in Sevens are the ideal preparation for the XV-a-side game. Now Sevens tournaments are held all over the country, to the betterment of the game. Melrose will always be the doyen of the art, in memory of Ned Haig its founder (who actually hailed from Jedburgh), but all the other Borders Sevens – and Twickenham! – are real crowd-pullers – and very happy social occasions to boot. And *mirabile dictu*! The SRU even has its own full-time Sevens squad, touring the world under Melrose's Rab Moffat, and doing pretty well. And it's great to see that the third generation of the Crawford building firm in Melrose, the home of Sevens, have sponsored an international Youth Sevens to be held at the Greenyards. I played rugby with members of the first generation (Jock and Jim) and the second generation (Adam or more popularly 'Yid'). The third generation, John or more popularly 'Choppy', served with the KOSB in Malaya and, as well as running his building empire, is an enthusiastic veteran.

The Melrose Sevens are sacred. All attempts by the SRU or Edinburgh District to change the date have failed miserably and they are now firmly fixed for the second Saturday in April every year – commonly known to Melrosians as the right time to plant your seed tatties. The Irish go for St Patrick's Day, but that's a bit early for the Borders. An invitation to the Melrose Sevens to a team outside the Borders is taken, worldwide, as a huge compliment.

I played in the Melrose Sevens only once – for London Scottish – and suffered the humiliation of being knocked out in the first round by Edinburgh Accies. The Coutts family can claim only two Melrose Sevens 'medals' – my mother presented the Ladies Cup to Gala in 1937 and my father officiated at Adam

(Ned) Haig's funeral at the Wairds cemetery on the slopes of the lovely Eildon hills.

Is nothing else sacred in the world of Rugby? Apparently not. At the back end of 2005 a group of English men and possibly women actually made a bid to buy out *the Barbarians*! The 'Baa-Baas' are the very Holy Grail of Rugby Football. To receive an invitation to play for Baa-Baas is *almost* more prestigious than an invitation to Melrose Sevens. Founded in 1890 by W. P. Carpmael of the famous Blackheath RFC, it became the first rugby side to play important fixtures in the Midlands and later to arrange memorable Easter weekend tours in South Wales, playing a warm-up at Penarth on the Friday, Cardiff on the Saturday, Swansea on the Monday and Newport on the Tuesday. This was the occasion for International players, latterly from all over the world, to realise that the guys whom they were knocking bits out of a week or two before were really human and extremely nice people. I had the rare privilege of playing with them for three seasons. The Committee and those of the party who were not playing used to sing from the stand every try the Baa-Baas scored:

> It's a way we have in the Baa-Baas,
> And a jolly good way too.
> For the rugby game we do not train
> But we play it with a will.
> It's a way we have in the Baa-Baas
> And a jolly good way too.

Not very brilliant but handsomely appreciated by the Welsh crowd.

It is probably very difficult to find now, but those who are interested in the Barbarians, and particularly those rascals who wish to take it over, should get hold of a copy of its updated history 1890–1955 by the illustrious Andrew ('Jock') Wemyss, who played rugby for Scotland before the First World War with two eyes, lost one in the war, and played rugby again for Scotland with one eye after the war. He was a wonderful raconteur and also rugby commentator on the BBC ('the Scottish forrits are no' playin' verra weel the day'). In his history he recounts his meeting with Adam Robson of Hawick at London King's Cross, on their way back from Adam's first Easter tour in South Wales. Adam, obviously somewhat overawed in the presence of such a senior Baa-Baas committee man, exclaimed in the railway carriage: 'Oh, what a marvellous tour that was', to which the seasoned Baa-Baas veteran replied quietly: 'I've never known a dud one.'

The Barbarian officials have a great reputation for longevity. There have only been five Presidents in their 125 years: W. P. Carpmael, Emile de Lissa, H. A. Haigh Smith ('Haigo's going to buy us beer'), Brigadier H. L. G. Hughes ('Hughie') and, until recently, M. R. Steel-Bodger ('Mickie'), the effervescent English captain, who has enlarged the club to its worldwide proportions today. To those who would destroy this unique club with all its international friendships I would say – LAY OFF!

The long-awaited breakthrough that Scotland needed so badly arrived on the *Sabbath* (my father would have been horrified), for on Sunday, 5 February 2006 at 4.53 p.m. Scotland beat France, consistently the best team in the Six Nations Championship, twenty points to sixteen at Murrayfield. It was a magnificent game. At last Scotland's backs have learned to take the ball going flat out, not standing still. It was a great pointer to the future.

If you want to make true friends for life, join a rugby club.

Family reunion, Kinross, 1954

Family reunion, Kinross, 2005 – see how they grow!

Chapter 4

THE FAMILY

The real Golden Thread of life is, of course, family and I count myself lucky to have a remarkable one. On 23 October 2005, my younger daughter, Sheena Fleming Coutts, organised a clan reunion in Kinross of all the Couttses and Murrays who had stemmed from the marriage of my parents 'Jack' Coutts and Rose Fleming. Thanks to email and Sheena's incredible enthusiasm, no less than eighty-three people were eligible and fifty-one attended. Here is the story of the progenitors of that clan and some of their offspring.

My father, John William Coutts, was born in Manchester in 1876, the son of Robert Coutts and Jean Henderson. He must have been an extraordinarily bright student, for he graduated BA from the University of Manchester at the age of eighteen and MA at twenty-one. He then went to the Glasgow Free Church College and the University of Göttingen, Germany, in order to become a minister of the United Free Church of Scotland. That might seem a strange decision for someone brought up in Manchester, but his family were Presbyterian to their roots. He did his assistantship in Glasgow Hillhead, a place that would become very well known to the family, and he was called to his first parish at Coldstream, Rodger Memorial UF Church. As a bachelor he lived in some style, of an evening driving with his pony and trap to dine with one of the local lairds, demolishing a bottle of whisky (not considered excessive in these days, just hospitality) and returning with the pony knowing the way home better than his master. (In the next chapter I have described Dad's character as seen through the eyes of his five sons.) He had a lovely sense of humour. Coming back from an evening service in Glasgow he passed a 'close mooth' and heard a distressed lady say impatiently: 'Och, haud ma Bible, Jock, I'll tak' them doon masel'.' Despite his fine academic brain he could never come to terms with the internal combustion engine. Just east of Amulree he wanted to turn down via Trochry to Dunkeld. He completely misjudged the right-angled bend and went straight through a hedge into a lady's garden. He was so charming and apologetic that the lady almost apologised for having her fence in the wrong place! His 'missus', whose car it was, forbade him from driving again.

After just a year in Coldstream he succumbed to the family urge to travel and accepted an overseas posting to Rangoon in Burma. A memento of that tour was a beautiful silver table napkin ring, which he left to my wife Morag because she was the only member of the family who had also been to Rangoon. Next he was called to Ferryhill Church in South Aberdeen. Within a year he had the infernal cheek to ask the daughter of the Lord Provost, Sir John Fleming, to be his bride – and she accepted! How did he do it? I suspect that he would have been invited as matter of course to preach at the upmarket church of Beechgrove on the north side of the river, where Sir John was an elder.

There is a very fine stained glass window now in Beechgrove, presented by Lady Fleming, in memory of Sir John, who died in South Africa in 1925.

His bride, Rose Fleming, was one of a large family. She was called 'Rosie' by her parents, and all the contemporary photographs depict her as real beauty. She lived to be 100 years old and was a superb mother and grandmother, although my sister Maisie always claims that she really wanted six boys. Rubbish! It must have been quite a change for her to move from fashionable Rubislaw to a more humble part of the Granite

City. It was her first experience of a manse, the traditional home of Scots ministers. The Session Clerk called to see if she wished any alterations after the previous incumbent. She trailed round the house, listing all the improvements she would like to make in painting and decoration. The Session Clerk was very patient, but when they got back to the front door he had to admit: 'Well, the Session have given me authority to spend one pound'! Throughout her marriage, it was the custom that the minister's wife should automatically be President of the Women's Guild. She never complained. She was a great 'mixer' and used regale her husband with all the amusing sayings that her ladies contrived in the vernacular. She particularly enjoyed her time in Melrose, where she could enjoy riding at Selkirk with her bosom friend from Milngavie, Jan Orr. Encouraged by Jan, Granny Rose is the only member of the family to have ridden the Selkirk Common Riding. Eilidh Walker, the wife of the Headmaster at St Mary's School, was another close chum. They shared the same affection for the Border tongue, quoting ladies at a picnic saying 'Ah'm fair sweetin' eatin', 'It's a handy thing a caur,' and so on. She was in her element as chairman (no chairwomen or chairpersons in those days) of the Women's Home Mission Committee of the Church of Scotland. She made a point of visiting the hundreds of Scots girls who went down to East Anglia every year to gut the fish. Their hands got in a terrible state with cuts and they were constantly bandaged. She made a great hit when she addressed the Annual General Meeting in a full Usher Hall during the Church of Scotland's General Assembly week. She fired on all cylinders, brought the house down and achieved a headline in the *Daily Express* – 'Star of the Assembly', no less. My brothers all said how fortunate we were to have had parents who enjoyed public speaking. Mother told me she never read her speeches. She prepared them in writing and memorised them – and if you miss something out – bad luck. She said she could see the print in front of her eyes as she spoke to the balcony. She wrote down her Memoirs, wittily entitled 'Horse Trot to Moon Walk', and I hope that some day one of the family will knock them into shape and publish them.

Both my parents came initially from crofting families, the Couttses from Tarland, Aberdeenshire, and the Flemings from Glenshee, as described the Preface to my book *One Blue Bonnet*.

After the appropriate interval, a family was soon on the way and early in 1910 their first son, Bobby, was born. He proved not to be of a very strong constitution, and one day when his mother was pushing the pram under a railway tunnel she pointed up and said: 'Look at the chuff-chuff.' He paid no attention and it was subsequently discovered that he was stone deaf. What a terrible shock for a young mother to discover that her first-born was deaf. She blamed it on her total ignorance of pre- and post-natal preparation. How brave they were to start again. Typically, she told the story about the Women's Guild member who said to her several years later, 'With six kids, Mrs Coutts, are you a Roman Catholic?' 'Oh no,' she replied, 'it's just that every time Jack hangs his breeks over the bed-end I become pregnant'!

Undaunted by Bobby's deafness, they made superb arrangements for him to lead a normal life despite his disability. He went to the Deaf School in Glasgow, Dad's next posting – or should I say 'calling'? Bobby did so well at the school for the deaf that the principal said he could do no more for him – he was lip-reading so well that he could go to the Glasgow Academy with his brothers. This he did and he loved it, including rugby at the Anniesland playing fields. People asked him: 'How do you know when the ref blows his whistle?' 'What a stupid question,' he would say. 'Because everything stops.' Simple. His lip-reading was so good that he could tell what people were saying behind him through the reflection in his glasses. Many's the clip on the ear I have received for speaking out of turn. Funny how the talents are distributed. No one else in the family could knock a nail in straight – but Bobby was a natural engineer, with a 'pair of hands' that could fix anything. A kindly elder arranged for him to do his apprenticeship with the old Albion Motors in Clydebank and he went on to enjoy a full career in Scotland and England. He was a fanatical member of the Boys' Brigade. After the war he became Captain of the Earlston Company when he was working there for Brownlies, the timber merchants. I still meet Borderers who remember him. I went to help him in camp at Rhu on the Clyde one year, and told him, after Lights Out, that there was a helluva row still going on in the tents. He went tent-slapping with his swagger cane and assured me that all was now quiet. Not so. Bedlam. Deafness can sometimes have its benefits. He married Enid, also deaf, and it was good to see their daughter and her talented children at the Kinross reunion.

It was brave indeed of my parents to 'try again', but as there were no contraceptives (known to them anyway) I suppose it was inevitable. Anyway, Walter Fleming Coutts was born in Aberdeen on St Andrew's Day 1912, so it was appropriate that he should be the first of several members of the family to graduate at St Andrews University, where he distinguished himself by being elected President of the Students' Union and travelling in an open landau with Field Marshal Smuts, our much-admired opponent in the Boer War, who had been chosen as Chancellor of the University. He won his rugby blue at St Andrews and a half blue at Cambridge, where he and, later, our brother Philip prepared themselves for the Colonial Service in East Africa. His early service as a District Officer in Kenya soon caught the attention of the High Heid Yins and his promotion was rapid – Chief Secretary in Kenya, Administrator in St Vincent and Grenada in the Caribbean, then Governor and finally

Governor General of Uganda. He was much decorated and I had the great privilege, as his 'cadet', of carrying his banner as Knight Grand Cross of St Michael and St George for the full length of St Paul's Cathedral when it was laid up after his death in Perth, Western Australia. He had retired there with his wife Jinty, son Dave and daughter Jacqueline (Kel), who is still homesick for Scotland and charms us as often as she is able with her presence.

What can I say about brother Ben, 'Mark 3', who was born in April 1916 while Dad was in France? Ben and I (born two years later) were both 'war babies' and living proof of the soldiers' query: 'What's the second thing you do when you go home on leave, Jock?' Easy – 'Ye tak' yer boots off.' Ben? 'I lo'ed him like a very brither.' Well, of course he was my brother but the good Lord has a way of making us all slightly different. And Ben was different; in fact he was remarkable. He found school and Vet College a struggle, but was determined to be a farmer so he started on the bottom rung of the ladder by learning to be a groom at a prosperous stud farm in Sussex. The only way he could enjoy a summer holiday (no EU regulations in those days) was to join the Territorial Army and have a fortnight in camp, which employers were obliged to recognise. The local Regiment was the Sussex Yeomanry, who had recently said goodbye to their gee-gees and converted to Royal Artillery 25-pounders, the workhorse of the Second World War. They saw gallant service against the Italians in Eritrea. This was followed by Ben's commissioning back to the Regiment and almost immediately a near-fatal wounding in the face at Tobruk. Then came a whole series of skin-graft operations in Egypt and the UK. His journey home was on the ill-fated torpedoed *Laconia*, crammed with Italian prisoners-of-war, and he survived many days in an open boat. In hospital at East Grinstead, under the world-famous surgeon, Sir Archibald Macindoe, he joined many of 'the Few', RAF pilots who had done their bit for the Battle of Britain and suffered grievously. 'Archie' formed the Guinea Pig Club and persuaded them to live a normal social life in the local pub. Archie and Lady Macindoe became family friends. After the war, Ben got his wish to be a farmer in Perthshire (twice, at Lawhill and Woodburn), in Laggan Bridge (Gaskbeg), and in Argyll (Cairndow), as factor to the Secretary of State, Michael Noble, at Arkinglas. The while, he wrote seven books on agriculture, all in light-hearted vein, and broadcast on farming affairs for BBC Scotland for over fifty years. Did I say he was different from the rest of us? You can say that again.

He was a noted after-dinner speaker, speaking without notes like his mum, which some people think comes naturally. No way. It means a lot of homework and usually a rotten night's sleep before and after. I only once got the better of him. He was always desperate to become President of the Smithfield Show in London, an honour denied him, but he made Vice-President – and to his dismay had to say Grace in rhyme at the Annual Dinner. He had never explored the fun there is in rhyming verse *à la McGonagall* and he turned to me for help. For the price of a bottle of Grouse I produced this for him:

> O Lord who blessed the loaves and fishes
> Look down upon these Smithfield dishes;
> Good meat we feel you also blessed;
> Thou knowest all that beef is best.
>
> These hundred years we've nurtured it
> And always sought a tastier bit;
> By breeding, culture, elbow grease
> We've shamed grain farmers' life of ease.

God bless our pigs and tasty lamb;
Cunningham* couldn't give a damn;
You cannot beat a piece of pork
A-sizzling while you pull the cork.
So let us praise our pigs and sheep,
Though prices offered make you weep.

Through wars and drought and BSE
We've helped to keep our country free,
We've battled with the Min of Ag
And now it's Brussels' feet that drag.

God bless our members near and far,
E'en those who lingered at the bar;
You turned the water into wine
These guys will turn it back agine. [English pronunciation]
And if you've blessings left to spare
KEEP SMITHFIELD GOING FOREVER MAIR.

---

* Cunningham was, presumably, Minister of Ag and Fish.

Ben's stories and jokes, both in books and speeches, were the topic of many an auction mart throughout Scotland. They were mostly 'clean' and the one I liked best was the story that he told in his thank-you speeches on various occasions.

Geordie, the orraman, was due to extend his feein' for another year and as he sat, invited from the bothy, to have his 'tea' with the farmer and his wife, he was asked: 'Why are ye no' signing on, Geordie?'

'Is it the bothy, Geordie?'

'No.'

'Is it the food, Geordie?'

'No.'

'Is it the pay, Geordie?'

'No.'

The Big Bla' – the massed pipes and drums of the eight regiments of the Scottish Division beat Retreat on the Horseguards Parade, London, in the presence of Her Majesty the Queen in 1969

Two Highland colonels – the late Colonels Tommy Lamb, Queen's Own Highlanders (Seaforth and Camerons) and Colonel Claud Moir, Black Watch (right) – two of my closest friends

After fifty years as Colonel-in-Chief of the KOSB, the Duchess of Gloucester receives a ceremonial drum from Lieutenant Colonel Colin Grant Hogg at Fort George, near Nairn

Lieutenant-General Sir William Turner (right) meets Regimental Sergeant Major 'Dusty' Smith
of the Coldstream Guards at a Passing-Out Parade at Oswestry in 1962

The future NCOs and Warrant Officers of the Brigade of Guards and Infantry of Line proudly
march past the Inspecting Officer after two years of training

Soldiers of the KOSB pictured in 1945
Left to right: Colour Sergeant George Walker, me, Sergeant 'Stoor' Richardson and
Sergeant Wat Linton

The Inter Scaldis Pipes and Drums at Berwick-on-Tweed

The old Royal High School – it would have been the ideal location for the new Scottish Parliament (photo courtesy of Michael Wolchover)

The new Scottish Parliament building, Donald Dewar's dream – wrong place, wrong design, wrong price (photo courtesy of Michael Marshall)

The Melrose team who won the Melrose Sevens in season 1947
Back row, left to right: R. R. Brown (Secretary), T. Hook, A. Crawford, H. Stuart, A. Lyal (President)
Front row, left to right: A. Frater, J. Cassie, J. Simpson, D. Hogg
(photo courtesy of Jack Dun, Melrose RFC)

The Kelso team who won the Melrose Sevens in 1986
Back row, left to right: Douglas Robeson, Euan Common, Bob Hogarth, Andrew Ker and,
standing, Roger Baird
Front row, left to right: John Jeffrey, Gary Callander and Eric Paxton
(photo courtesy of the *Southern Reporter*)

The old Murrayfield – here crowds of 100,000 would gather to watch amateur rugby
(photo courtesy of SRU Library)

The new Murrayfield – with seats and accommodating 67,000 spectators who now watch
professional rugby, the stadium is not always filled (photo courtesy of SRU Library)

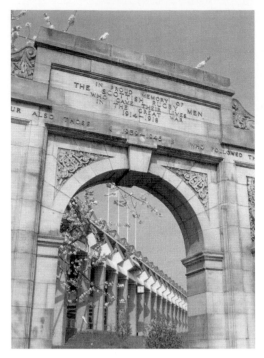

The Murrayfield War Memorial

Lorna Antonini, granddaughter of the presenter of the Calcutta Cup, shows it off to Watsonians' Scott Hastings (left) and Hawick's Colin Deans

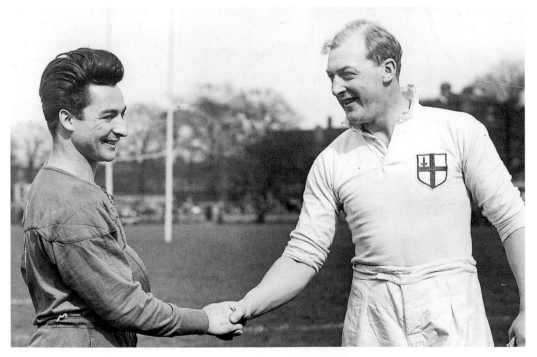

The entente cordiale – here I am in 1948, as captain of the London rugby side, shaking hands with my Gallic counterpart before the start of the annual London v Paris game

'What is it then, Geordie?'

'It's jist that no one ever said, "Weel done, Geordie!"'

So I say, 'Weel done, Ben.' And over 500 people said the same in St John's Kirk in Perth at his Memorial Service. And not a few said, 'We'll no' see the likes o' him again.'

Like us all, he enjoyed his dram. Discussing 'opening time', I always insisted that 'the sun was over the yard arm' at 6 p.m. 'Na, na,' he said, '5 p.m. in the winter – the clocks go back on Sunday.'

Alas, poor sister Maisie, spirited into this world on St Patrick's Day 1921 in St Luke's Manse, Milngavie. From the start, life was tough, having to compete with four elder brothers who were not accustomed to feminine ways. She found a real partner when her wee brother, Pip, was born. She was devoted to him. The family move from Milngavie to Melrose hit her unfavourably. From the Park School in Glasgow she had to become a boarder at Esdaile, the College for Ministers' Daughters in Edinburgh, where she was home-sick and unhappy. She left in wartime, a thoroughly unsettling period. Her strength was in her extraordinary artistic ability. Our wise parents saw that her future lay in the world of art and obtained a place for her at Bedford College, where she was very much respected. Always modest to the point of disparagement about her artistic ability, she did in fact have several exhibitions of paintings and sketches, which have been widely admired. She married her boyfriend from Melrose, Jim Murray, home from Burma with a Military Cross from the Chindits behind the enemy lines. I had the honour of piping them from the pic-turesque Dundurn Kirk at St Fillans to our home at Rath Erenn, three houses away – a short bla'. Under difficult circum-stances she raised a family of five, but sadly had little time to develop her outstanding artistic talent.

Mark 6, Philip Gordon Coutts was also born in Milngavie, on 20 Aug 1924. Granny Rose, rather naughtily, described him as 'the Virgin Birth'! To use that grossly overused expression, 'he was a lovely man', and we were great buddies, especially when we played in the second row together for London Scottish. He was educated at Glasgow Academy, St Mary's, Melrose, Fettes College and Jesus College, Cambridge, and was a fighter pilot in the Royal Air Force. With all that behind you, you should do well in life, and he did, as far as his short life permitted. He was a workaholic. After early retiral from the Colonial Service in Uganda, he became a most proficient executive of the Scottish Wool Boad. He stood for and won his seat in both the Clackmannanshire District Council and the Central Region Council. As an elder of Dollar Parish Church, he returned one evening from a meeting of the session, laid his head on the table and died at the early age of fifty-seven. He had followed brother Wally into the Colonial Administrative Service, first as Assistant District Commissioner in Soroti, Uganda, and later on tours of duty in Mbale Entebbe College and the Secretariat in Kampala. Next he set up and ran a college for African chiefs – a significant achievement in the time of Prime Minister Harold Macmillan's famous 'Wind of Change' speech of 1960, which signalled British approval for African independence. Independence in Uganda brought him back to Scotland as the front man of the Scottish Wool Board. He married a chum of Maisie at Bedford College, the cuddlesome Alison, whose large family was the only branch to achieve a one-hundred-per-cent turnout at the Kinross reunion! Their children, Alastair and Catriona, were a good advertisement for the benefits of boarding school education which is inevitable for overseas families. Both educated at Dollar Academy, Alastair is a top surgeon and Catriona a proud mother and a much-loved Church of Scotland minister, at Cumbernauld Old Parish Church.

Honours in the Family:
GCMG, KCMG, CMG. CBE, OBE, MBEs – four, DL, Boy Scouts gallantry award, Boys' Brigade gallantry award.

So, five sons and only a niece wearing a dog collar . . . Why? Read on in Chapter 5.

The late Donny McLeod (photo copyright of BBC Photo Library)

Chapter 5

UNDER THE INFLUENCE

The following is a transcript of the BBC Radio Scotland programme *Under the Influence*, broadcast in June 1974.

Voiceover introduction: Donny McLeod talks to five sons of
the manse with not a dog collar amongst them and asks them
about the influence their home had upon their lives.

Ben: Well, one didn't see a lot of Father during the week, he
was a very active and hardworking minister. I can't remember a
single evening back in the old Milngavie days when one saw
Dad at night so that, like all families, Mother had a lot to do
with actually sending us off to school and we saw Father in the
holidays. A tremendously warm character, very human, with a
wonderful sense of humour. A very tolerant father when you
think of five ruffians like us for whom he'd given up smoking
and drinking for our education and benefit. It's his warmth
that I'll probably remember.

Donny McLeod (DM): Ben Coutts, one of the five sons of
the late Reverend Dr John W. Coutts recalling the personality
of his father and the influence their upbringing had on the
whole Coutts family.

Despite the fact that none of them have followed directly in
their father's footsteps by entering the ministry, the imprint of
their manse upbringing has remained with all of them.

Bobby, the oldest brother, is totally deaf. Throughout our
discussion he lip-read all that was being said and I asked him
how he had been influenced by his parents.

Bobby: My father always went out of his way to make quite
sure that I was taking part in the life of everybody. I'm very, very

grateful to my father for his religious views and I would like to mention that he was a most broad-minded man, especially for his day. Of course in the early days we weren't allowed to do anything on Sunday but to read the Bible and any religious material, but as time grew on he relaxed his views and we were able to go further afield in our own ways. Also I have been helped by the influence of my four brothers here, at school and at home.

DM: Frank, as one of the younger members of the family, how much do you remember of your mother's influence? She must have been extremely important with your dad away so much. How much of an authoritarian and disciplinarian was she?

Frank: Well, she was the Sergeant Major of the family . . . she still is, going strong at eighty-six. I support what's been said about Dad's humanity. The man was a saint! I mean, if you look back at his record, there he was churning out sermons Sunday after Sunday and not just ordinary sermons – they were brilliant! Three hundred and sixty-five days a year, he was living his life as a minister, but when I say he was a saint, he was a very earthy saint. How he put up with this family of six rumbustious kids storming around the manse defeats me. But the study was sacrosanct and it was as much as your life was worth to go near it. But when you did get in, there was a tremendously warm welcome and a very happy atmosphere.

DM: Pip, on a practical note, stipends being what they were in those days and with six hungry mouths to feed, were times tough for you at any time?

Pip: No, I think that somehow, I don't know how, both of them managed to do their utmost for us at all times and I was never aware of any form of deprivation at all. I also owe a lot to these other four as well as to the two parents, and indeed to my sister Maisie who was my chum at our stage of the thing. One strong point of attachment for is me is that Dad was a great musician and from him I acquired a great interest and love of music.

Frank: Wally was the famous gourmet. He was always quoted as saying, 'There's only two days in the year when I'm properly fed: one's my birthday, the other's Christmas.' Sunday evening in the manse was always a very pleasant time after all the tensions of the day were over, and quite often Dad was away 'visiting Minister'. This particular Sunday there was a Heeland gentleman – he'd been preaching at the evening service – and we all went back to the manse for supper. We sat round the table and the Heeland gentleman was very slow in the speech and he was cracking away with Mum and the rest of us were sitting round tucking in and after about ten minutes Mother looked across at the visiting Minister's plate: he hadn't had a thing to eat and there was *nothing* left on the table *at all*, and nothing in the larder either!

DM: The gannets had descended! Ben, you were recalling a time when rugby played an important part in the family's activities?

Ben: We all loved it, all sorts of rugby stories told. The one when two of us were playing for Melrose and there was a terrible swearing match went on and a lovely Border wag said, 'Ah, there go the Meenister's sons!' I always remember Archie Craig who is dearly loved by the Church of Scotland and a great friend of the Coutts family for years. He was in Glasgow University as the padre at that time and used to come and play rugger with us on the lawn. We had a neighbour who was very anti the Coutts family because we were always kicking the ball into his vegetables and then running across it, I don't blame him now, but then we thought he was a terrible chap . . .

Wol: We ruined his gooseberries!

Ben: That's right! We kicked the ball over and we said, 'Oh we can't go and get the ball now', ba's bust, game's jiggered sort of thing, and Archie said, 'No, no, no, I'll go over and talk to him as Christian to Christian.' And Archie was away about ten minutes and he came back and said, 'I think that fellow's the Devil!'

Frank: Dad loved his dram and on one famous occasion during the war, we had a lodger staying with us . . . go on, Ben.

Ben: There was this half bottle and I'd brought it back. I'd got on to the quartermaster or something, wangled it for Father and this was going to be a great celebration. This was the day of corks in whisky bottles, not screw tops, so Dad in that lovely Highland way said, 'There'll be no use of this tonight' and chucked the cork in the fire. Whereupon this 'lovely' Mr Baird came along and knocked over the half bottle, and Father . . .

Frank: Censored!

DM: A family tragedy! Wally, did you feel as a son of the manse that there was anything expected of you, more than was expected from the son of the man next door, that because you were the Minister's son, you had to be an example?

Wol: Oh, yes, indeed. Once you had become sixteen or seventeen it was a case of teaching Sunday School in the morning, then going to the service, going to the Bible Class in the evening, and then going to the final service at the end of the day. But that was never put upon you, it was by and large through leadership.

DM: Ben, was there any sort of feeling of having the Bible rammed down your throats and reacting against it in any way?

Ben: No, very far from it and I know this question is going to come out sooner or later: why didn't one of us join the Church? I think it was that Father's feeling very strongly was, and Mother's still is, that there's a tremendous job to be done in the Church of Scotland as a layman and you'll find that four of us here are Elders and do our part as best we can with all our faults and haven't we got plenty of them.

Frank: I would go further. I think as time went on the compulsion eased, and by the time I was in my teens, there was definitely no compulsion to go to church. But by that time the seed had been sown and you felt you ought to go and you

joined the Boys' Brigade and all the other Church organisations because you were a son of the manse. I don't think one
was penalised for it, I can't remember at school being seeded
out as a son of the manse and being expected to be a goody-
goody as a result of it.

Pip: I think all of us around this table would have to admit
that the thought had crossed our minds. I think I would have
had a crack for the Church if I'd been a little more certain of
myself at the time and as Ben has said we've all got doubts and
it's no good having faith unless you've got doubts first. And
probably the War had something to do with that, I think those
six vital years may have made a difference to our thoughts at a
time when we might well have gone towards the Ministry had
it been the piping times of peace. But it wasn't.

DM: Ben, you raised the point. Did it ever occur to you to
join the Ministry?

Ben: Yes, very strongly. When I was in my late twenties I
had a bad experience during the War getting my nose blown
off and then landing up on a raft on my way home and a few
other things we can forget about, but it gave me a burning
faith which had gone though a nasty stage before. I don't
think anybody at this table or anybody who goes to church
and really believes has not gone through Doubting Thomas
periods, it's bound to happen. I'd gone through a stage of
working as a groom on a pretty tough job where chaps
seemed to be getting a perfectly good life and never went near
Church. They had a lot of fun that I didn't seem to appreciate
because we'd been given a sense of duty by Father and
Mother and were told there were certain things we were
expected not to do, and one began to wonder whether religion was what it was cracked up to be. So I went though this
doubting stage, then came the War, and then this experience
and I came back terribly keen to do something more active
for the Church. Father looked me straight in the eye and said,

'Well, you couldn't pass your exams at school, I don't suppose you can do any better now,' and that was that. And he was right, because he said, 'Look, you start talking about Hebrew and things of this sort, you've got to have the background.' I do the odd lay service now and I find that not having this background of education is hopeless. They gave us the chance, but I didn't take it.

Wol: I'm certain of one thing: Father would never have expected us to go into the Church unless we had the call. This was his whole belief in life and I remember as a youngster saying to myself, 'Well I can't see the call much', but nevertheless felt that he was absolutely right in this. I also went though a stage of agnosticism between the ages of twenty-one and thirty-one, where I virtually believed in nothing. After that I feel that the training, the grounding that one got in the manse stood one in great stead and I'm a firm believer now and have been for many years.

DM: Did any of you have what's usually called 'the Road to Damascus' experience, a moment of conversion, one moment when your doubts or agnosticism left you and you decided to make a complete change in your life? Obviously that experience on the raft for you, Ben?

Ben: Not a blinding light, no, I'm not one of these people who says, I walked across London Bridge and then I was suddenly hit between the eyes. I think it was very gradual. One has a lot of time to think when you're in that sort of position, however, and you suddenly realise what is right and what is wrong. You can't always live up to it.

DM: Frank, your experiences in the Army, did they help to confirm or at any time shake your faith?

Frank: I think confirm. And answering the question about becoming a Minister: as all the others have said, Dad always made the point, I can't decide this, it must be decided from within. And I think as far as careers were concerned, you've got to look back to the '30s and remember it wasn't choosing a career in these days, you were finding a career, you were hunting for a career . . .

Wol: How right you are, you were extremely lucky to get one!

Frank: And you had to have one of two things, some money to get to university or a heck of a lot of ability and I had neither. But coming on to the wartime, when you eventually get into a hot situation, it brings you face to face with the realities of life and I think like so many others during the War that my faith was enormously increased and eventually completely confirmed.

Ben: Just imagine that period in the '30s when Wally had got through varsity, you were a bobby on your flat feet in London and I was a groom with a crowd of thoroughbreds, lordy, they must have been proud of us, mustn't they! I mean after that education they gave us that this is all that we could do at that time. And yet, you see, their faith pulled them through. They gave us the grounding that allowed us to get off the springboard eventually.

Wol: Father never earned more than £600 a year in his life and in the end, in the last ten years, he went to Melrose on half that salary because he felt he'd done the job that was required of him in Milngavie. I can't really think of many people would do that nowadays. It was extremely tough on Mother and I reckon that that was faith.

DM: Bobby, how much of a help were your parents to you with your deafness at that time? Deaf children today are helped a great deal by the system. How much of a help were your parents in their attitude to your deafness?

Bobby: My father decided to send me to the Academy for an experiment for six months and I wasn't quite sure what kind of reception I would get. First of all they made arrangements for me to sit in front of the class, with the teacher in front. After the end of six months, I told my father I liked the school so much and I would very much like to stay on if it was possible and I spent four very happy years at the Academy.

DM: And played rugby football.

Bobby: It was marvellous!

Wol: I have the most terrible conscience about our sister. I think we treated her absolutely terribly. I can remember an occasion when we dangled her favourite teddy out of a window in the hope that she would shriek for it.

Frank: Oh, she had her uses, you know. We used to make her goalie always. I always remember at the holiday home in St Fillans we used to have wonderful fun out the back there, playing rugger sevens and football. You always needed numbers and Maisie was always put in as goalie. She was known as Sparra.

DM: Wally, you went on to become a colonial Governor in a very dramatic part of the world when you were there, and one which has stayed in the headlines ever since and come into it again with the Ugandan Asians being expelled. How did the kind of upbringing that you had had stand you in stead when you were in East Africa?

Wol: I have absolutely no doubt: it was the background that one got from the family and if I can put it in one word I hope without being 'pi', it was integrity. By integrity I mean that you kept your promises and that's the sort of thing I felt we were taught in the manse; if you promised something, you stuck to it.

DM: Pip, there was another point brought up, as well as integrity, and that was a sense of duty being a son of the manse. Did you feel the wider implications of a sense of duty?

Pip: Yes, this is a thing that's so ingrained in us we'll never shake it off. Sometimes we curse it. I'm sure all of you round the table at times say, 'I wish I could get rid of this conscience that continually plagues me,' and there are times when we'd like to throw it out of the window and do what seems to be pragmatic at the time.

DM: Frank, what was it that sparked your interest in the Army?

Frank: Dad had been a padre in the First War with the Royal Scots. I wear his Sam Browne to this day and it's got the worn mark on the leather at the back where his hymn books hung. When I spoke about becoming a regular soldier, Dad gave me tremendous encouragement and the home qualifications that we've all spoken about. Wally's used the word already: integrity.

Wol: Still fighting with the Devil!

Frank: Yes! It was a tremendous assistance, particularly I think in dealing with soldiers. The background of the Kirk was a huge help because all our congregations were classless. You were dealing with people from top to bottom the whole time.

Ben: I think that's one of the biggest points of the lot. Dad could go into Buckingham Palace, or I remember him very well in '26 when he took me down to Clydebank when things were really bad. He was helping out a fellow Minister because Dumbarton presbytery was in with Milngavie and I'll never forget it, a man showing him his hands and saying, 'There's ten fingers there and there's no job for them.' Dad had that tremendous gift of 'talking to the Jocks'. He talked about the days when he used to play cricket with the Earl of Home and Dad and he were opening bats and they were the only two who had ever taken back the Coldstream XI sober when they'd won against Berwick. But he talked about him as though he was an ordinary chap, as he would talk about a shepherd. He had a tremendous ability, as has Mother, of mixing and I think that this is essential, especially nowadays.

Wol: I support Ben on this. It's seen me through an awful lot of difficulty in life.

DM: Ben, you talked about your father saying that there were other ways of serving the Church, other than becoming a Minister, that the layman was important. Have you been able to prove that yourself?

Ben: I've been an Elder in four different churches and a Session Clerk in one; I've preached on a good few occasions. I feel it is essential that laymen do back up the Church of Scotland and I don't think it is getting enough backing from its lay people. I was at Presbytery last night and some of the very learned were talking about things that are impossibly impractical: this is where those of us who have lived an ordinary life may help. I've lived along with shepherds, with ghillies, with very tough grooms in racing stables, with soldiers and in the Sergeants' Mess, as have the rest of the boys in this family, and you then know how the other chap ticks and if you can bring this into the Church in any form at all then I think we are doing what Father and Mother would like us to do.

DM: Pip?

Pip: Yes, I'd support that. Like him, I've worked in a couple of parishes as an Elder and sometimes I'm a wee bit disheartened perhaps by the Churchianity that seems to be going on without the Christianity. There was a fallow period, I lost everything for about ten years in my twenties, but when I became thirty and had children of my own and that's a very important point of course, then you begin to realise all the questions that your own parents were asking, then perhaps I began to give a little and take less.

DM: Frank?

Frank: Yes, I think the Army offers a very special and different challenge; in active service, as I've already mentioned, you've got the challenge and even in so-called peace, I've been very mixed up in the Irish situation. One way and another you come face to face with the challenges of Christianity. But as well as these challenges, we also have tremendous benefits. We are brought in very close touch with the padre and we're able to give him, in stations at home and abroad, a great deal of assistance. I think in this way I have enormously enjoyed the experience of offering what I had to offer with my manse background, and was ordained as an Elder in Singapore and was able to join the Presbyterian congregation there. I think for all of us, attendance at kirk has become a part of our lives, it's not a thing that you force yourself to do, you just do it as of custom.

Wol: Sunday without kirk to me is just not a Sunday. I was aiming fairly high, I wanted to become Chairman of the Governors of the BBC! As I happened to know Lord Reith I wrote to him and said perhaps he might back my application, which he did I believe, but in setting out to him what I thought I might be able to do, and listing administration and all the rest of it, he came back with literally a single-line letter saying, 'Yes, I will help but what you learned in your father's manse will do you much more good in the BBC than anything else you know.'

DM: A classic Reithian response! I suppose the most awkward kind of question that one can put now is the influence that you've tried to exert on your own children.

Ben: Oh, it's time up, Donny!

DM: Very difficult subject to broach. Frank, how difficult was it for you?

Frank: Very difficult but like our parents we just tried to set them an example and I think slowly, like the dripping tap, the message begins to get through.

Pip: We had a sort of rule which we stuck to pretty closely during term time although we let the brakes off a bit during the holiday until they were fifteen, sixteen, I suppose, and then they made up their own minds as to whether or not they were going to Church. I don't think either of them are regular Church attenders now but they're certainly, again, not anti. I think they are highly critical of what they see as an inward-looking sort of congregation of people who go along to sing a few hymns, say a few prayers and then go home and forget all about it for the other six days of the week. I accept this criticism, I think they're dead right, but when we have talked about it, I've said, 'OK, come in and join it and change it for us.'

DM: Wally, could I ask you, and all of you, to sum up what we've been talking about: how your parents, the manse and growing up in Scotland in that era influenced you, your career, your action through life?

Wol: Without the influence that I had in the manse I could not have done what I have done in my life.

Ben: Absolutely the same. The ease of mixing with people. Father used money when he had it, he never had it, but he was always saying to us, you can't take it with you. I think we've all got this, we've enjoyed the things money can give us from time to time but not one of us has made big cash and we've never worshipped it, which everyone seems to do nowadays, and this is directly from that background.

Frank: I think we've hit only one or two points of the tremendous benefits we all got from our parents. I'm a believer in heredity and the home background. I believe I owe everything to my parents.

Pip: It's bedrock stuff, it must be said again, this question of integrity, of sense of duty, of the conscience, the driving force in our lives has come from that manse, and we're deeply, deeply grateful for it because we couldn't have led any sort of life without it.

Voiceover: In *Under the Influence* Donny McLeod met five sons of the manse who did not follow their father into the Church – Robert Coutts, Sir Walter Coutts, Captain Ben Coutts, Brigadier Frank Coutts and Philip Coutts – and discussed the influence of their home in the manse upon their chosen careers. The producer was Douglas Aitkin.

Looking back over the past thirty-two years, my views haven't changed. Growing up in a manse family, religion was very much an everyday thing and we really didn't think too much about it. It was simply a part of our lives. As the next chapter will reveal, my views on religion have become a little jaundiced. Nevertheless, I am still a firm believer. I have taken to the pulpit on many occasions but usually on Remembrance Sundays and, sadly, when giving eulogies for departed friends. Various religious revivals over the centuries prove that it is always a live issue and I have tried to set down my views of the Kirk during most of the twentieth century honestly. Because of my chosen career they are naturally Army-orientated.

'Oldies' invariably consider that things were better 'back then'. So many changes in the Kirk do annoy me. I know that the ministerial dog collar must be an irritation in these days of open-necked shirts and no ties but it is their uniform after all and they should at least be proud to wear it at the Assembly. How else can we differentiate between ministers and elders? Home visits by over-worked ministers are now very rare. 'Welfare' is offloaded to either professional or voluntary workers. How about spiritual welfare? Sad, too, to see so many fine church buildings fall into disrepair and then be reused as furniture storerooms etc. When labour was cheap, it was fashionable to put up finely architectured kirks with spires going higher and higher to seek heavenly contact. But the cost in maintenance? Enormous. Money which should be spent elsewhere.

But never mind, to the tune of a Salvation Army band, 'the Church goes marching on'. It comes and goes in spasms. Moody and Sankey's rollicking hymns had the Victorians humming them, Billy Graham's crusades certainly brought them in (even to Murrayfield! – I was there) and now Dan Brown, even in fiction, has set people thinking seriously about the life of Jesus Christ.

Colinton Parish Church (photo courtesy Dr D. J. Whyte minister of Colinton Parish Church)

Chapter 6

RELIGION

Part I: As It Was

In a manse family back in the 1920s and 1930s, religion naturally started at Mother's knee. We wouldn't have dreamt of sitting down to any meal, however humble, without someone saying Grace – even when all six of us were rushing for the 8.21 to Glasgow. (A recent history of Milngavie quoted a householder in Strathblane Road as saying, 'If you see the Coutts boys running past your window there's no point in going for that train!') Nor would we go to bed without saying prayers. Initially they took a standard form: 'God bless Mummy, Daddy . . . then a catalogue of the whole family and friends, the cat and the dog . . . and make me a good boy/girl. For Jesus' sake, Amen.' In due course we were expected to expand in accordance with our own way of life. Prayer played a very important part in our lives. No one ever defined what amounted to 'sins'. Boys naturally assumed it was something to be ashamed of like masturbation.

There was an obvious temptation to turn prayer into a wish list. So far they had been very selfish, all 'one's needs and desires', without a thought for the other fella. Prayer is a bit like horse racing. You win some and you lose some. For example, hundreds of soldiers must have prayed as I did: 'Please God ensure that those German shells whistling overhead land on another Battalion and not on us.' And after the war perhaps: 'Thank you God for understanding my desire to sleep with that gorgeous bird last night and please be a good chap and ensure that she doesn't become pregnant.' Things changed when we had responsibility for the lives of others. Vows were taken seriously. Joining the Church was an individual choice. I chose to make it an away fixture (London, 1937) so as not to give the impression that I was being ordered by my dad. There followed marriage (1948) and the eldership (1960).

No school started the day without prayers, ours so sincerely led by Dr Edwin Temple (Ted), now lying peacefully in the cemetery at Comrie. Prayers didn't stop even on holiday. After breakfast there were always ten minutes of prayer in the sitting room – three-line whip, including even Ally, the maid. It was then that one came to admire the conviction of my father: his religion was not confined to the pulpit. He carried it into every home in the parish and shared it with the unemployed during the hungry '30s. No let-up on Sundays. As brother Wally has described in *Recollections of a Scottish Childhood*, we worshipped before the Union of 1928 in the United Free Church, just east of the shop at St Fillans, now a private house. After the Union we all sensibly worshipped in the charming Dundurn Parish Church. The minister was the Reverend Duncan McLaren, who hailed from Stranraer. Speaking with an accent which became very familiar to me in the Regiment, he frequently referred to his former Parish of Trinity Gask as Trinity Gaask-er. This invariably sent the manse pew into uncontrollable giggles. The organ, before electricity, was pumped by the lady organist's feet. This caused her backside to wobble dramatically, a further cause of merriment. Swimming and boating were forbidden, but the health-giving walks enabled us to relish the countryside in one of the most beautiful corners of Scotland.

With all this prayerful activity, it was something of a shock to go to the Boys' Brigade, which we all did, apart from Wally who chose to be an upmarket Boy Scout, to find that most people did not run their lives like this. A week in camp, sharing a tent with boys who came from desperately poor homes, enabled one to 'see the other side of the coin'. Boys' organisations have had a bad press recently, and the officers of all organisations, some with little formal religious training, faithfully took the Bible Class and taught the young generation the basics of the good life. The good they must have done, and are doing, to Scottish society in general is incalculable. My eldest brother, Bobby, who was born totally deaf, held every rank in the BB until he finished, after the war, as Captain of Earlston, where he is still remembered.

Sunday worship came naturally. With no television and radio in its infancy, it was the 'done' thing. Father's church was packed every Sunday morning and reasonably full in the evening too. Habits die hard. Sunday without church is unthinkable. Even when Ben was roughing it as a stable-boy in Sussex, when I visited him for a weekend we invariably went to the English church – and found to our dismay that we were refused Communion. It was good for our education. People weren't all like us. If the Christian religion is to survive it has a long way to go in ecumenical endeavour. However, Church of England chaplains in the Army were more broad-minded than their civilian counterparts.

Looking back, I count myself fortunate indeed to have had an upbringing of this nature. As the years went by, things changed, as they always do.

Part II: As It Is Now

Considering our manse background, it was not surprising that we should all become attached to the Church of Scotland wherever we landed up – and between the six of us we landed up in a heck of a lot of places! And, in whatever capacity, our grounding in the Kirk never left any of us, as we expounded at some length in the last chapter.

As most of my adult life was in the Army, my religious

observance was within the Army system, where every unit, by long tradition, has a padre or chaplain, of one denomination or another; in the case of Scottish Battalions, almost always a minister of the Church of Scotland.

There is a long history of religious observance in the British Army. The Royal Army Chaplains' Department was founded in 1660, and they have provided chaplains of all denominations with coverage of every unit. Their duties in peacetime are similar to those of any parish minister: church services, baptisms, weddings, funerals, visitation of the sick and assistance to the Commanding Officer and officers in maintaining the morale of all ranks, sometimes in very difficult circumstances.

In war they play a very special part when battle is joined. They have to arrange for those who are killed to be buried, usually in close co-operation with the Commonwealth Graves Commission, whose beautiful cemeteries are located all over the world. Sometimes chaplains became involved in the actual fighting. Over the years they have won an astonishing number of Victoria Crosses for outstandingly brave conduct in the face of the enemy. One padre, the Reverend Theodore Bayley Hardy, was awarded the VC, DSO and MC. Until the Second World War, church parades were always compulsory. I did not hear many complaints. The officers took the same view as the Scottish missionary in Africa who, as he walked down the aisle dispensing the incense, intoned: 'If it'll dae ye nae guid, it'll dae ye nae hairm.' The services were spoiled by the Sergeant Majors, who took the opportunity to get companies on parade far too early and inspect everyone, particularly those 'employed' men who crept out from nowhere once a week. So the Platoon Sergeants would get their platoons on parade even before that. Then the officers arrived and more inspections took place. Eventually it was a relief to get to church and have a quiet kip. I think it was Field Marshal Montgomery, a devout Christian, who realised, about 1942, that Sunday was a day of rest and the soldiers should enjoy it the same as everyone else when operationally possible. Church then became voluntary, with the officers and their families setting a good example and the Duty Company sending along a few pressed men to supplement those soldiers whose conviction encouraged them to attend. As in civilian life, the non-attenders, when crises like funerals arose, expected the services of the padre as of right. 'Twas ever thus; I have known several highly intelligent men who have never given a thought to the Church but whose next of kin come to me and ask me to find a minister to bury them.

Officers, for the most part, whether believers or not, looked on themselves as Regimental Christians and supported the padre at voluntary church parades – services actually; they were not parades. They attended church and their wives particularly appreciated the opportunity to have their children attend Sunday School.

The padres I had the privilege of working with during my time in the Army were: Ronald Selby Wright, Moderator of the General Assembly of the Church of Scotland 1972; Neville Davidson, Moderator 1962; Frank Findlay; Tom Nicol; Robert Greer – not a chaplain but an ex-Japanese POW in Singapore; Farquhar Lyall; Matt Robertson; Walter Evans, Church of Wales; Gerry Murphy, Church of Ireland; Bill Johnston, Moderator 1980; Robert Craig, Moderator 1986; Jim Harkness, Moderator 1995, who was previously Chaplain General; Alan Main, Moderator 1998; Haisley Moore; and John Shields. Tom Nicol, a special chum from school onwards, became chaplain to HM the Queen at Balmoral and Gerry Murphy did the same at Sandringham. Walter Evans wrote a very amusing little book called *Evans Above*. Bill Johnston was our own family minister in Colinton from 1965 until he retired in 1992. He married both of our daughters – Fiona in 1975 and Sheena in 1989. His sermons were a joy and, on the way home, my wife Morag used to say, 'I wish he had gone on a bit longer.'

The large number of Army chaplains who have been nominated and selected to be head of the Church of Scotland is evidence of the great regard in which their work with our Forces was appreciated by the fathers and brethren of the Kirk and the people of Scotland generally.

As General Secretary of the Royal British Legion Scotland, it was naturally one of my duties to give Remembrance Day addresses, very often from the pulpit. On 6 November, 1979, I had the privilege of giving a Remembrance address on BBC Scotland. Here it is, for the use perhaps of subsequent holders of that office:

> Last Saturday I was standing on the beach at Flushing in South Holland, remembering the landing of the 52nd (Lowland) Division there thirty-five years ago. What were the thoughts running through the minds of my comrades from the Borders – and when I say 'comrades' I really mean comrades without any political connection – standing there bare-headed in the cold November sunshine while Jim Coltman from Hawick played the 'Floo'ers o' the Forest are a' Wede Awa"? Each shared his own memories, but undoubtedly we thought of Malcolm who was killed soon after the landing, and of Ken who was there on Saturday – with no legs at all.
>
> For all ex-sailors, -soldiers and -airmen it is a sad occasion. We recall the young faces – 'they shall grow not old as we that are left grow old' – and we could recall that their lives were wasted when we see the opportunities for peace which have been lost, when we see our ex-enemies economically – and perhaps morally? – stronger than we are, and the brotherhood of man rent by divisions too deep to penetrate.

But all was not gloomy on Uncle Beach. Although war is a hateful thing, to be rejected as a means of national policy, we looked at the bright side. A continent had been saved from a monstrous tyranny, and in a town which had been put to the sword rich and lasting friendships had grown up between the Lowlands of Scotland and the Low Country of the Netherlands; economically and militarily we were united in a way that perhaps might have averted Hitler's war if we'd shown enough vision.

This all makes sense to my generation, but what of the young listener? Well, there's plenty for that generation to think about; they don't hesitate to join the forces of law and order and the record of service in *international* strife is the admiration of us all.

So Remembrance is for everyone – not only on Sunday to make a conscious act of remembering with gratitude – but also to make this a time of practical remembering. I reckon that one family in five in Scotland is still affected in some way by the results of conflict and there are still many wounds to bind up. At Poppy Time let us all make an offering for . . . those people and their dependants who may be in distress as a direct result of one of the World Wars or one of the many other engagements since . . . to war pensioners in their struggle through the Legion to obtain their share of the national cake – at long last the imposition of income tax has been removed from our widows' pensions in recent months . . . and particularly at this time the housing of ex-servicemen and women who now seek sheltered accommodation in the evening of their lives.

So we remember at our war memorials, and we make a practical act of appreciation to those who have served and those who are still serving – for they are the ex-servicemen and women of the future. But most of all in 'Lest We Forget' week, *we remember the relatives of the fallen* and re-dedicate ourselves to the belief that, in God's name, it mustn't be allowed to happen again.

When you see the poppies fall from the roof of the Albert Hall, falling gently on the heads of our young servicemen and women, I hope that you'll think on these things – and remember.

I suppose I had always accepted the rudiments of our faith without questioning them. During my service I had recourse to worship with the Church of England and much enjoyed the glorious English of the Common Prayer Book. But I didn't stop to think of the words I was mumbling. Their refusal to permit us to take Communion rankled.

One day I was shocked to hear my mother say, 'I don't believe in the Resurrection.' This gave me cause to look more closely at the Creed. Nowadays I find that I produce more 'la-las' than words when we say the Creed. I have now come to the conclusion that I believe only in God, Jesus Christ and the Holy Spirit. Everything else is froth. Thousands of words have been written by scientists trying to convince us that there is no God. As far as I am concerned they are wasting their time. There is definitely some extra-terrestrial force which created the universe with all its wonders and which runs our lives. It is the Holy Spirit which tells us instinctively the difference between right and wrong. Full stop.

I am not prepared to argue about the truth of the New Testament with anyone who has not been to the Holy Land to see for themselves. I was fortunate indeed to be invited by that great man Bernard Fergusson, Lord Ballantrae, to succeed him as President of the Friends of St Andrew's, Jerusalem, that lovely church, conceived in Edinburgh in 1919 by two Elders in St Cuthbert's and opened in 1930. This gave me the opportunity to visit the Holy Land from time to time and to see for myself the evidence that the Gospel story is true in all its essentials. How could anyone not believe in Jesus who had visited the charming chapel 'Dominus Flevit', where Jesus 'wept over Jerusalem', walked the Via Dolorosa and – most of all – sat in the garden where the stone was rolled away. The evidence is there for all to see and has been accepted by Christians everywhere for 2,000 years. It is the same in Galilee, where we used to go on pilgrimage to the Hospice (now the Church of Scotland's only five-star hotel). Once we spent a weekend in a small room cooped up during the Jewish festival of Yom Kippur when one was liable to be stoned on the streets. OK, there are inconsistencies. We swam in the lake and tried walking on water – without success – and ate loaves and fishes at the vulgar cafés on the waterfront.

But I accept these parts of the Gospel story as 'spin' put out by the Alastair Campbell of the day, trying to justify the message which this remarkable young man was putting across wherever he went. I put the miracles in the same category. After all, miracles do happen and I feel sure that Jesus was looked up to as a sort of first-century Billy Graham, winning hearts wherever he went.

Many parts of the story I cannot accept. I do not believe in the Virgin Birth. This was a cover-up. Virgin births are physiologically impossible. Crudely, I have to believe that, in soldier's parlance, Joseph – or someone else? – 'had his leg over' nine months before and it was a bold decision to travel to the City of David in her condition. I can accept the basic accommodation, 'no room in the inn', the straw and the donkey. Wise Men are two-a-penny in every generation. I'm not strong on astrology but I'm prepared to admit that some religious zealot believed that the star did guide them to the place where Jesus lay. I don't agree with angels – not 'up-a-ky' anyway. I believe that angels are right here among us – nurses in our crowded hospitals and people doing good works in thousands of charities. Same for

Heaven. I don't believe that Heaven is up there, it's down here. The good God gave us all one lifetime and it's up to us to make it heavenly or hellish. Heaven to me is Melrose winning their own Sevens, walking round Loch Muick on a summer's day or sexual bliss at any time. Hell is here too; examples might be a night in the Combined Assessment Centre at the Edinburgh Royal Infirmary, having to listen to a heavy metal disco, or being beaten 50–0 in the Calcutta Cup at Twickenham. Nor can I, as I said before, agree with the Resurrection. After 2,000 years those 'many mansions' must be full to overflowing. 'The hole in the side', yes. But lifted up to Heaven? Sorry, nothing doing. More spin.

So there. I'll probably be excommunicated.

Part III: The Kirk

I have nothing against the Kirk. The 'United Free' were very good to my father and he was a happy man when the Union was achieved in 1928. Fancy having three different Churches of Scotland in a wee place like Melrose – ridiculous; now happily sorted out. Really, our forefathers must have been an argumentative lot. They must have had precious little else to do but argue about how many angels could stand on the sharp end of a needle!

I am a complete religious conformist and not a religious zealot in any way but there are three faults in the organisation of the Church of Scotland which 'get my hackles up'. First, there is no command structure. Second, there is no discipline. Third, the system of appointing ministers to a vacancy is outdated and ludicrous.

Fundamentally, to claim that all ministers are equal is rather illogical. I'm sorry – we're not born equal and everyone in this world has a boss except Church of Scotland ministers. It is ridiculous to say that a Moderator, be it of the General Assembly or a Presbytery or a Kirk Session, is the first among equals.

They must have authority and for a considerable period. It is palpably embarrassing when the Church of Scotland is asked to make a statement on some controversial subject. Moderators are obliged by the system to say that their opinion is only their own opinion and they cannot speak for the Church. It makes the Church look silly when other religions, particularly the Roman Catholic Church, come out with a clear opinion because they have the authority to do so. Sorry to speak in military terms but the Moderator, having been duly elected (by the 'old-boys' network' – those of Conservative leanings need not apply), should be the Commander-in-Chief for a set period of years, not just one. This may be elitist but at least the Moderator could say, 'This is what the Assembly thinks – I'm the chap they have chosen to speak for them.'

The Church lacks discipline. Ministers go their own way without any check on their performance. Well, there is the quinquennial visit. Under the Old Pals Act a nearby minister comes along and says to the incumbent: 'You scratch my back and I'll scratch yours.' Every minister should have a Confidential Report each year, written by the Moderator of the Presbytery, who also should have an increased authority. These should be submitted to 121 George Street, where the office of Ministers' Careers would be overseen by a senior minister of the Church, say a retired Moderator of the General Assembly. Moderators at every level should be appointed for a fixed term, probably five years and extendable.

I have had the good fortune to hear this subject discussed in my father's manse. Going back a long way, I can recall the views of George MacLeod, in his heyday at Govan and Iona, James Stewart (whom we had the privilege of introducing to his charming wife, Roz), Archie Craig, and, more recently, Ronald Selby Wright, Robin Barbour, Bill Johnston, John McIntyre and Robert Craig. Archie Craig was the one who saw our failing most acutely and he had the courage to raise it in the

General Assembly. Unfortunately, he used the word 'Bishops' instead of 'Moderator' and that put a lot of backs up. The question no longer seems to be on the agenda and we go bumbling on with some totally inadequate ministers – *Carry On, Padre* – being undetected and unwanted by their congregations. In this day and age of permissiveness and openness, it is difficult to find anyone with enough smeddum to raise the question once more in Presbyteries and the Assembly. Oh how I wish I were younger!

Likewise, the system of appointing a minister to fill a vacancy is antiquated and absurd. At least Kirk Sessions now can start the process when their minister is still serving. For generations the procedure didn't start until long after the minister had retired, leaving congregations to wither. After a laborious process in Presbytery, a church is given permission to engage a new minister for *x* number of years – not a promising prospect for an up-and-coming minister with a young family to educate. Permission granted, the congregation then have to elect a vacancy committee consisting of thirteen members 'in the face of the members and adherents'. For Pete's sake, why thirteen? Three wise men or women could do the job perfectly well. The unlucky thirteen then go charging around the country in large cars – it's always persons with large cars who land up on vacancy committees – and they scour the country for parishes miles from base, seating themselves around in each kirk in an attempt to conceal the fact that they are a vacancy committee. Who's kidding whom? Regular church attenders can spot a vacancy committee a mile off. After consuming a great deal of petrol they eventually decide on some hapless individual and report back to Presbytery, who will probably put all sorts of objections in the way of their decision.

This system could be greatly shortened if the committee for Ministers' Careers was involved at an early stage. They will know from their computerised profiles who the most suitable minister would be for a particular parish. They will know which ministers are ready for a change, say after the average period of twelve years in post. They should know of those who seek a change and others who ought to be given a fresh start, always assuming they are acceptable to the vacancy committee. It would save a lot of petrol! Advertising in the Church of Scotland's magazine *Life & Work* was originally considered to be rather vulgar but it seems to me to be perfectly sensible and logical.

Here endeth the lesson.

This is the Army padre referred to on page 84, the saintly Canon Gerry Murphy,
a former Irish rugby internationalist

Chapter 7

THOUGHTS FOR THE DAY

I have laid bare my views on religion in the last chapter, but this was not my first opportunity to do so. Thirty years ago, having done quite a lot of public speaking, I was invited to take on the daily 'Thought for the Day' slot on BBC Scotland which then went out at about 7.50 a.m. each morning. At that time, it was rudely known as the 'God slot' and was usually given by one or other of the well-known ministers in Scotland. I accepted and decided to ally my thoughts to my experiences as an Army officer in various situations. I had never had any difficulty in speaking into a mike but these programmes had to be scripted to last for exactly three minutes. It meant writing and rewriting, practising with a stop watch and the inevitable struggle to sleep before the alarm went off at 6 a.m. for a 7.30 arrival at the BBC offices which were then in Queen Street, Edinburgh. No cup of tea was offered to amateurs – just a gruff, 'You sit there and speak when the red light comes on.'

This is a transcript of my week's endeavours.

Monday

Good morning! I'm sure a lot of men who listen to this programme will be shaving at this time. There could be a few cut chins right now when they hear a Brigadier announced for 'Thought for the Day'. Maybe you'll think it's a Salvation Army Brigadier. Come to think of it, there was a distinguished Salvation Army General of the same name, but I certainly couldn't aspire to the dedication and compassion of that body.

No, it's a soldier. I've been a sudger for thirty-seven years. And I want to talk about things that soldiers think about. Soldiers think? That brings to mind the one about the Army officer who was so stupid that even the other Army officers noticed it.

But soldiers do think, you know. On this ice-cold morning the soldiers will be standing shivering in sangars and on draughty street-corners in Northern Ireland – and they'll be thinking all right. I visit that unhappy land from time to time and I certainly go along with that politician who said, 'No one should ever say or do anything which will make matters in Northern Ireland worse.' Amen to that. Life there for the soldiers is tense – it can also be boring – but things happen suddenly, and when they do that's when soldiers think – hard. The realisation that that guy there is out to kill you – that's when you begin to think about the deeper things in life.

When I was commanding a battalion, the padre said to me – the padre is what we call the minister in the Army – the padre says: 'Right, Colonel Frank, you are in the pulpit next Wednesday morning – five minutes on why I believe in God.' And the padre was an Irishman too – a saint if there was one – and an Irish Rugby International to boot, and he wasn't the kind of chap you argue with. So he got this soldier thinking – and thinking hard.

At that time I'd become very keen on gardening and I never ceased to marvel at the miracle of planting one seed potato on St Patrick's Day or thereabouts and in the autumn sliding my spade into the soil and bringing up ten or a dozen golden tatties. That's productivity for you. But man never made a spud. Despite all the wonders of modern science, you challenge any professor to make a potato in his laboratory.

So, that's what I said to the troops. And I also said I believe in God when I see a newborn babe, wonderful in every detail of the human body. And I believe in God when I see the sunset in the Western Isles, or a thunderstorm in the Malayan jungles.

And what did the troops say? They gave the accolade – the highest praise a soldier will ever bestow – 'Nae bad, Sir.' And what did the Sergeant Major say? Well, you'll have to listen to the next instalment for that.

So that's my thought for you on this Monday morning: 'Who made the first spud then?'

Tuesday

Good morning! The news this morning made pretty grim reading. G.R.I.M. – an expressive four-letter word. They seem to be in vogue again. That reminds me that I was telling you yesterday about the Sergeant Major and you maybe connect Sergeant Majors with four-letter words. Well, you couldn't be further from the truth because today's Sergeant Major is an educated man who doesn't need foul language to exercise his authority.

This Sergeant Major I was telling you about was a Warrant Officer Class 1 in the Coldstream Guards – a magnificent figure of a man and a born leader – and the padre said to him: 'I want you to read the lesson in church next Sunday.' You've never seen a human face so contorted with shock and indecision. But he was equal to it and he came back with: 'All right, Padre, but only if you allow me to take my pace stick up to the lectern.' Now the pace stick is that muckle great piece of timber which the Sergeant Major tucks under his arm and when it's opened out it measures exactly the right pace for marching on parade. And that's his symbol of authority; he just wouldn't feel right without it.

There are lots of examples in civilian life of symbols of authority – the lollipop man seeing the kids across the road would be a forlorn figure without his lollipop; the football referee would be in a fine pickle without his whistle; and at sea think of that imperious ring on the engine room telegraph which instantly achieves a reaction to the captain's commands.

And 'command' is the operative word. There's not much point in having symbols of authority if they don't mean anything, and that means obedience or – dare I use the word? – discipline. I would be a rich man if I had a pound for every time people have growled at me: 'What this country needs is a return to National Service – and a bit of discipline.' Well I won't be drawn into that argument, but I think everyone would agree that most ventures in life need leadership and management. Unless you're really at the top of the tree, everyone in life has a boss who is expected to exercise leadership – with or without a symbol of authority like the Sergeant Major.

That great leader, Field Marshal Bill Slim, had a perfect definition of leadership: 'Whether you command ten or ten million the recipe for leadership is the same – it's a mixture of example, persuasion and compulsion.'

There is an organisation in Scotland which has a superb symbol of authority – an anchor. I mean, of course, the Boys' Brigade, founded by Sir William Smith, coming on for 100 years ago in Glasgow. The BB gives a great lead to countless young men, And it's an inspiration to hear 100 lusty young voices singing:

> We have an anchor that keeps the soul
> Steadfast and sure while the billows roll.

And very many people – 951 million, according to the Sunday papers – owe allegiance to a leader whose symbol of authority was even simpler – a cross. That leader demands a way of life which has weathered many stormy seas. And what's more, it has stood the test of time. So my thought for the day is: 'We really can't run a ship without a Captain.'

Wednesday

This week I've been talking about soldiers and the things they think about and maybe you think I've painted a rosy picture of life in the Services, with chaps going round all day thinking about their Creator and discussing leadership. Don't get me wrong! The Armed Services are just a reflection of the rest of our community; they are made up of good people, a few bad people and their fair share of indifferent people. They're all human beings and subject to the same ups and downs as everyone else.

One thing I can't give them good marks for is their language. Oh, it's a fair . . . gosh, I nearly said it! On the other hand, you can say about soldiers that they are on the whole happy people. In the words of that overworked quotation from a gravestone in Baltimore, they 'strive to be happy'. And there are four-letter words that make them happy.

The first is W.O.R.K. As you creep off to work, rushing your breakfast or yawning your head off in the car, this may be no time to be lectured about the dignity of labour. But give thanks to God that you are in work. And give a compassionate thought for those who are not. Maybe this is the day when things will improve for you. I know a man who says he loathes every minute of every working day. Now I could understand this if you had to howk coal out of the earth, stand in a fish shop all day long with freezing fingers, or if you had to get up at four every morning to do a milk round.

Yet people, most people, are happy at their work. On my way to work each morning I pass a milkman with his cuddy and two helpers and by that time they're munching their morning piece outside the Scottish Land Court in Edinburgh. They look as happy as Larry – so much so that visitors often stop and take photos of them, though I expect it's the cuddy that is new to them. Work is surely a most important ingredient in the pursuit of happiness.

There are other four-letter words which bring happiness in life – P.L.A.Y. and H.O.M.E. and L.O.V.E. They all play their part. A church could help to bring happiness to your life. It's available in all denominations and men and women have been saying for centuries that it is their belief in God which holds the true key to the art of living. So my thought for today is: 'There are plenty of four-letter words; how many can you think up on your way to work today?'

Thursday

Good morning! I've been accused of being too hearty with my 'Good mornings' – even woke someone up! (I thought that was the whole idea of the thing.) But my mood today is sombre because of the number of tragedies which have been reported in today's news.

Even in so-called peacetime, soldiers have their own share of sadness and a lot of separation from their families. But one of the compensations of a soldier's life is the tremendous sense of comradeship which comes to the fore when a tragedy strikes.

I was privileged a few weeks back to attend a church service in Belfast when a Scottish Infantry Battalion was unveiling a stained glass window in memory of their comrades who had given their lives in Northern Ireland. It was a very moving occasion. The service was voluntary but the kirk was packed – everyone from their smart regimental uniforms and tartans to those in combat kit, with the grime of the streets still on their clothes, their faces grey with fatigue – all of them gathered together as a regimental family and united in sympathy for their mates and compassion for the next of kin.

During the service, as I looked around at the strong faces of those Scottish Borderers, I couldn't help thinking of the weeks and months of patient peace-keeping they'd been through, Among all the unpleasantness there are so many tales of kindness and compassion. Down in a back street of east Belfast an old grandmother living on her own welcomed the soldiers to her home night after night. And when the soldiers left, they wrote a tribute in Scots which was framed and handed to her. It may have been nearer McGonagall than Burns, but it came from the heart:

> Aye, auld gran, ye are a 'stoater';
> O that there is nae doot,
> Ye tak us in while winter's cauld
> And never throw us oot.
>
> Ye bake yer tarts and drappit scones,
> The sudjers for tae feed.
> And tak them tae yer ingle neuk,
> Ne'er leave a man in need.
>
> Weel, Gran, it's noo for auld lang syne.
> It's time to say guid nicht.
> God kens, he'll keep ye richt.
> For me, we'll help ye wi a' oor micht.

Heart-warming stuff. And, in my present appointment in the British Legion, I see that same spirit of comradeship and compassion again among the ex-service community in Scotland. There's so much to be done. The Welfare State seemed to have all the answers but – surprise, surprise – someone discovered that welfare is nothing unless accompanied by the compassion and caring which keep it alive. As the cares of the needy become aware to us – the elderly, the disabled, the homeless, the lonely – you may feel that it's all too much for you. Then Burns has a word of encouragement: 'Wha' does the utmost that he can, will whiles dae mair.'

So my thought for today is the Legion motto, 'Service Not Self', coupled with the prayer 'Who needs me next, Father?'

Friday

Good morning! I've enjoyed sitting here every morning this week, hearing the daily news bustling round me – the devolution debate with the line humming between Glasgow, Edinburgh and London; the Rhodesia talks; the economy; Prince Andrew off to school in Canada – you name it, it all goes on here. The thing that has intrigued me most is the communicating technique of the whole thing. I'm a pretty untechnical sort of bloke and I've never had much luck with communications. I still can't understand how the telephone works and it wouldn't surprise me if my very voice put some gremlins into the Kirk o' Shotts transmitter. This goes back a long way, to the days of 2LO [the code name of the first British radio station] when my father was giving one of the first religious broadcasts in Scotland. The whole family was gathered round the primitive set with its vital cat's whisker – expectant, tense and alert. Out came a succession of whistles and crackles, and finally the doom-laden voice of the announcer: 'You have just been listening to a talk by the Reverend J. W. Coutts.'

Twenty years on and the scene turns to a battlefield on the west bank of the Rhine near Wesel. There was good deal of Teutonic aggro flying about and it was really terribly important to get through to the Gunners on the company radio set, the 'eighteen set' of inglorious memory. So I shouted across to my radio operator who was hunched up in his lit trench with his head barely visible above the soil, 'Is the set working, Borthwick?' Back came the reply with a Teri [Hawick] accent: 'Scotland's winning one-nuffin at Hampden, Surr.'

Nowadays Army communications are much more professional. They drive round in their Land Rovers, flicking from net to net and muttering slick and confident signalese, like 'Sunray for One Nine Alpha. Arriving your location in figures five minutes', which means that the boss is on his way – watch out and mind ye put the kettle on.

But communications for every man (every person? how dull) mean much more than radio communications. It means talking and listening and reading and writing and just getting on with our fellow human beings. How often we fail to understand something – or somebody – simply because we fail to make ourselves understood. It seems to me that the person who aspires to lead the Christian life has a special duty in this respect. The motto of His life was 'Love thy neighbour as thyself', and that surely means communicating in our daily lives without rancour and, if possible and appropriate, with good humour.

Is there perhaps someone today whom you ought to contact again – a letter, a phone call or a Christmas card? Remember, we're approaching the season of goodwill – and there's only two more weeks to go – as if you need reminding! At the end of this week's soldiers' thoughts, I'd like to pass a message of goodwill to Joanna Hickson and Douglas Kynoch through there in my native city – that's to say if you're hearing me! You are great communicators. Thanks a lot to you and the *Good Morning* team for the great job you do in bringing us happily through the morning hours.

And my thought for the day is 'For God's sake – keep in touch.'

All these years later it may be interesting for readers to compare them with today's 'Thoughts', which seem to be to be over-political and rarely religious. I received several very complimentary letters, but the one which really mattered was from the Religious Affairs Producer, the Reverend Ronnie Falconer:

> Dear Frank,
>
> Your 'Thoughts' this week have been terrific. I would have been proud to produce them. Well done indeed! And don't be put off by folks saying you were 'too hearty'.

It was precisely that cheerful quality that made the appeal to me and, I'm sure, many others. All good radio broadcasting is essentially being yourself – it is person to person conversation that counts. So good for you. Here's to the next time!

All blessings,

Yours aye,

Ronnie Falconer

The Colours of the 1st Battalion the King's Own Scottish Borderers are proudly held high as they march down the High Street of Edinburgh in celebration of the granting of the Freedom of the City in 1690

Chapter 8

ANOTHER REGIMENT LOST

After 316 years of service with the British Army, the King's Own Scottish Borderers, the 25th Regiment of Foot, is to be disbanded, along with all the other Regiments of the Scottish Division, and merged with the Royal Scots, the 1st of Foot on 1 August 2006.

Raised by the 3rd Earl of Leven in 1689 for the defence of the City of Edinburgh, the 1st Battalion of the KOSB will return from Northern Ireland to Edinburgh in 2006, in its new role as part of the 1st Battalion of the Royal Regiment of Scotland.

This chapter is not intended to be a history of the Regiment; that must be written by someone else, but, after thirty-nine years in the KOSB I would like to say adieu and put down some thoughts which may be of interest to contemporaries and possibly to the younger generation as well.

I have already said in the Preface and in Chapter 1 how foolish it was for the Government, represented by Mr Geoffrey Hoon, the then Secretary for Defence, to disband four of Britain's remaining forty Battalions of Infantry at a time when infantry soldiers are desperately needed in trouble-spots all over the world. If history is any guide, there will be a major crisis in the twenty-first century when Infantry Battalions will be required in large numbers. It will be then that the recruiters will call on young people to join a regimental family, linked to their own geographical area. People don't like to join 'the Army' as such; they want to join an organisation which recognises their birthright, their background, their skills and their aspirations. They know they will have to face danger and they want to do so with their pals from the same neck of the woods.

For the majority of my service, we have had the honour of having as our Colonel-in-Chief Her Royal Highness Princess Alice, the Duchess of Gloucester. Next to the Queen Mother, who was Colonel-in-Chief of the Black Watch, Princess Alice was the longest serving Colonel-in-Chief in the British Army, and certainly the oldest, for HRH lived to an astonishing 102 years of age. She loved visiting Battalions of the Regiment and attending functions in the Borders, as they reminded her of her youth, looking up to the Eildon Hills, which the Romans called Trimontium, from her holiday home at Eildon Hall – one of the loveliest views in Scotland. She obviously enjoyed hearing the Borders 'twang' and asking the soldiers where they came from. Although of a nervous disposition, she endeared herself to all ranks and the Regiment was truly grateful for the support we received. Of many memorable visits, the one which officers who served in Malaya best remember is when she landed in a tiny aeroplane at Batu Pahat in Johore, spared for a few hours from the Merdeka (Freedom) ceremonies in Kuala Lumpur. There were, inevitably, occasional hitches in the royal programme. When HRH was inspecting the Guard of Honour at the Freedom of Duns in 1972, it was suddenly noticed that she was wearing not the regimental brooch of the KOSB but that of her husband's Regiment, the 10th Hussars. Her dear friend and lady-in-waiting Dame Jean Maxwell-Scott quickly ensured that she was 'properly dressed' after lunch.

During the lifetime of the KOSB there have been only thirty-two Colonels of the Regiment. The word 'Colonel' does not carry with it any responsibility for discipline or command. It is an honorary title, unpaid, appointed by the Queen on the advice of the Colonel-in-Chief and the Regimental Trustees. The Army rank may vary from Lieutenant Colonel to Field Marshal. The Colonel holds no disciplinary or command powers but is responsible for the continuing ethos of the Regiment and, importantly, the selection of young officers, upon whose judgement the future of the Regiment depends.

The names of the KOSB Colonels in the following list indicate the wide nature of lifestyles over three centuries:

Rank and Name	Date appointed
17th Century	
David, Earl of Leven	1689
James Maitland	1691
18th Century	
William Breton	1711
Richard Viscount Shannon	1716
Colonel John Middleton	1721
John, Earl of Rothes	1732
Hew, Lord Sempill	1745
John, Earl of Crawford	1746
William, Earl of Panmure	1747
William, Earl of Home	1752
Sir Henry Erskine Bt	1761
Lord George Henry Gordon Lennox	1762
19th Century	
Hon. Charles Fitzroy	1805
Sir Henry Campbell	1831
Sir Henry Somerset	1856
Sir Henry Townshend	1862
General W. C. E. Napier	1882
20th Century	
Lieutenant General Wiseman Clark	1903
General Sir F. W. Forestier-Walker	1905
Lieutenant General Sir C. L. Woollcombe	1910
Field Marshal Earl Haig	1923
Brigadier General D. A. Macfarlane	1928
Major General Sir Edward Broadbent	1938

Major General E. G. Miles	1944
Major General J. Scott-Elliot	1954
Lieutenant General Sir William Turner	1961
Brigadier F. H. Coutts	1970
Brigadier A. D. Myrtle	1980
Brigadier R. W. Riddle	1985
Brigadier C. G. Mattingley	1990
Major General T. P. Toyne-Sewell	1995

21st Century

Major General John Cooper	2001

In the early days the Colonel actually owned the Regiment. Officers paid for their commission and the Colonel was responsible for providing the soldiers with clothing and provisions. It was a most inefficient system and the Government gradually took jurisdiction over all regiments.

The tenure of Colonelcy, certainly in modern times, is five years, but extendable. I was extended twice, once from five to seven, and then from seven to ten, a great compliment. Some Colonels were reluctant to give up! General Woollcombe, the grandfather of our most recent historian, Bob Woollcombe, having served for thirteen years, had to be persuaded to hand over to such an eminent successor as the Earl Haig of Bemersyde, fresh from commanding the British Army in France and busy forming the British Legion.

It is interesting to note that Sir Henry Townshend served for twenty years (1862–82) at a very crucial time in the Regiment's history. The War Office wanted the King's Own Borderers, as they were then, to be stationed in York, but the officers and the Colonel, after a long paper battle, persuaded the War Office that the Regiment should return to its Scottish roots – well, nearly – Berwick-upon-Tweed. Ravensdowne barracks in Berwick are the oldest occupied barracks in Britain, and were chosen as Regimental Headquarters and remain so to this day.

During the troublesome time of the '45 and the Battle of Culloden, three Colonels were appointed in three successive years, an indication of the turbulence then affecting all the forces loyal to the Crown.

Looking back at the achievements of the KOSB, the best indicator of their service is the roll of Battle Honours. These are not easily achieved. The majority of small wars, in which the Regiment has been engaged, do not merit recognition as Battle Honours. These are only granted for exceptional duty and usually when heavy casualties have been incurred. The decision to award a Battle Honour is considered at great length in committee before it is put before the sovereign for approval.

At a rough count, the KOSB have been involved in over 200 major battles during their service but only twenty-four Battle Honours have been awarded. These are:

The War of the League of Augsburg
The siege of NAMUR

The Seven Years War
The Battle of MINDEN

The French Revolutionary Wars
EGMONT-OP-ZEE

The Napoleonic Wars
EGYPT, capture of Alexandria
Capture of MARTINIQUE

The Late-Victorian Wars
AFGHANISTAN
Relief of CHITRAL
TIRAH

The South African War
PAARDEBURG
SOUTH AFRICA

The First World War

MONS, AISNE, YPRES, LOOS, SOMME, ARRAS, SOISSONNAIS-OURCQ, HINDENBURG LINE, GALLIPOLI, GAZA

The Second World War

DUNKIRK, ODON, CAEN, ARNHEM, FLUSHING, RHINE, BREMEN, NGAKYEDAUK PASS, IMPHAL, IRRAWADDY

The Korean War

KOWANG-SAN, KOREA

The Gulf War

The long Emergency in Malaya, which lasted from 1945 until 1958, was not awarded a Battle Honour.

The majority of these battles are not accorded memorial services. Those of the First and Second World Wars of course are, at the universally recognised Remembrance Day services on the Sunday nearest 11 November, when the guns ceased on the Western Front in 1918. Two unique memorials in the Regimental area still remain. Ex-servicemen in Hawick still gather at 'The Horse', a statue at the end of High Street, to recall the sacrifice of the many Borderers who lost their lives in the South African War of 1900–02. But, quite remarkably, after the passage of no less than 247 years, the KOSB still remember the outstanding bravery of their forebears, and those of five other Infantry Regiments and a Gunner Battery, at the battle of Minden in 1759, when Duke Ferdinand, the German Commander of the allied forces against the French, declared: 'It was here that the British Infantry earned immortal glory.' Each year over 100 Borderers meet at Berwick to celebrate this Battle Honour, wearing roses in their headdress to commemorate the fact that the Borderers of 1759 had put sprigs of (probably) heather (*Heide*) into their bonnets before the battle. These are the Golden Threads which have been torn apart by Mr Hoon and his Government in 2005–06.

There are so many other achievements to honour as the KOSB disappears into history. The custom of awarding the Freedom of Entry into cities or burghs goes back for centuries, obviously a much-cherished honour, which in military terms affords the right to recruit 'with bayonets fixed, colours flying and drums beating'. The King's Own Scottish Borderers have been accorded no fewer than eighteen Freedoms during their service. The first was in 1690 when the Regiment returned from the Battle of Killiecrankie, having been humiliated by 'Bonny' Dundee, the Highland Chieftain, who nevertheless was slain in the battle, on a hillside between Pitlochry and Blair Atholl. But Leven's Regiment, subsequently the KOSB, had defended Edinburgh from the Highland insurgents and subsequently fought honourably at Killiecrankie. There is no permanent record in the Edinburgh Town Council minutes of the granting of the Freedom but it is recorded that Leven's Regiment was given permission to beat drums (31 December 1690) and Baillie Grahame reported that the Privy Council had authorised the Earl of Leven to levy a company of foot for the Castle and to beat drums throughout the city and suburbs, an honour which the Regiment has frequently exercised by marching down Princes Street with 'bayonets fixed, drums beating and colours flying'.

Even the Terriers (the Territorial Army) didn't hesitate to take part in this honour. Two battalions, the 4th (Border) Battalion and the 5th (Dumfries and Galloway) Battalion were in camp at Dreghorn just before the Second World War broke out and they proudly marched down Princes Street before they went to war. On the occasion of the 300th anniversary of the KOSB the march down Princes Street was a truly memorable event, with contingents from all parts of the Regiment and from our affiliated Regiments in Australia, Canada, South Africa, the USA and Sweden.

Immediately after the Second World War a wave of loyalty

swept through the country. I was conscious of it myself. Home on leave from Germany in June 1945 I was asked to speak at a garden fête in Weirhill, Melrose. Very embarrassing. Every town and burgh was anxious to say 'thank you' for a victory well won, at one time very much against the odds.

Freedom Ceremonies

It was natural that Berwick-upon-Tweed, where the Regimental Headquarters of the KOSB has been located since 1881, should be first in line to honour the Regiment. Every town throughout the Borders had been 'invaded' by the Army for the six years of the Second World War. Some of the mills were used as makeshift barracks, every hall was requisitioned and many households were obliged to take officers and soldiers into 'billets'. The unfortunate Police Sergeant was the unlucky individual who had to 'invite' householders with a spare room or two to accommodate the soldiers. Many different Army Divisions spent long periods right across the border, including Norwegians in the West HQ in Dumfries and the Polish Armoured Division in the East HQ in Melrose.

But no town had as many troops to swell its population as Berwick. In peacetime there were seldom more than 300 troops in the ancient barracks; during the war this was increased tenfold to over 3,000, most being accommodated in the hastily constructed Magdalene Fields camp between the barracks and the sea.

Berwick-upon-Tweed: 7 August 1947

On a fine summer's day excitement ran high in the High Street with the crowds lining the pavements as early as 10.30 for a 12.30 parade. The 1st Battalion were abroad in Palestine and the 2nd Battalion, returned from Peshawar, had been put into 'suspended animation'. As a consequence, the troops from the Depot (Commanding Officer: Lieutenant Colonel L. F.

Machin) provided the Guard of Honour, commanded by Lieutenant Colonel Richard Henson. Princess Alice, the Colonel-
in-Chief, was to receive the Freedom scroll from the Mayor,
Councillor J. W. Carmichael. There was a fine turnout of VIPs:
the Earl of Home, the Lord Lieutenant of Berwickshire (who
met Princess Alice at Paxton Toll House, three miles from the
town); the Duke of Buccleuch, Honorary Colonel of the 4th
Battalion; and Lord Stair, Lord Lieutenant of Wigtownshire
and Honorary Colonel of the 5th Battalion. The Lord Lieutenant of Northumberland was prominent among the large
number of official guests.

After the inspection of the Guard, the Mayor referred to the
gallant history of the Regiment and stressed the very cordial
relations which existed between the officers and soldiers at the
Depot 'in sport, in charitable objects and in the general life of
the community'. He continued: 'In recognition of gallant services throughout a long and glorious history and to mark our
affection, the Corporation of this loyal and ancient borough
has been pleased to confer the highest honour which it is
within its power to bestow.'

The Colonel-in-Chief, in acknowledging this great honour,
displayed considerable personal courage – for the microphone
broke down and she had to read her speech all over again! Her
Royal Highness remarked on the notable hospitality of the
townsfolk who were always prepared to take soldiers into their
homes. After the march past, Her Royal Highness laid a wreath at
the War Memorial. The Army was represented by Major General
McMicking, Chief of Staff Scottish Command, and Major General Hakewill Smith, who had commanded two battalions of the
KOSB in the Second World War. Sharing the duties of preparing
for the ceremony with the depot was the Town Clerk, Mr R. B.
Davison. The Sheriff was Lieutenant Colonel W. R. Sprunt, who
had been Medical Officer of the 4th Battalion at the beginning of
the war – invariably known by his nickname 'Sprunto'.

Duns: 22 July 1972

The weather was unkind at the Freedom of Duns, but that did not prevent large crowds assembling in the Market Square to await the arrival of Her Royal Highness, the Duchess of Gloucester. Mercifully the rain stopped as Her Royal Highness arrived to be greeted by the Lord Lieutenant of Berwickshire, Colonel W. B. (later Sir William) Swan and Provost Tom Lennie. There was loud applause as the KOSB Guard of Honour, under the command of Major Allan Berry and led by the Pipes and Drums (Pipe Major Dennis Rodden), marched on to the Market Square where Her Royal Highness inspected the Guard, accompanied by Major Berry and the Commanding Officer, Lieutenant Colonel Bob Riddle.

In his speech Provost Lennie said: 'I often think of the different parts of the Borders as one big family . . . many of our Duns citizens have served in the Regiment which we in the Borders look on as our own . . . As a token of our gratitude to the Regiment we offer the Freedom of this old burgh, the highest honour that we can confer and, may I say, only the second in the history of Duns.'

In her reply, Princess Alice said: 'I thank you for the great honour which has been conferred on my Regiment . . . When one considers that the population of Duns is just a little short of 2,000 one cannot help feeling deeply moved that a town so small and yet so proud should wish to honour its local Regiment in this way.'

As Her Royal Highness laid a wreath at the Duns War Memorial, members of the 4th Battalion would remember that two of their most admired officers came from Duns – Jock Elliot, of Edington Mains, and Jim Bennet, farmer of Rulesmains. Jock was killed in action and Jim died of his wounds some years after the war. Two ministers of the Church of Scotland who had close connections with the KOSB were presented to Princess Alice: the Very Reverend Ronald Selby Wright, minister of the Canongate in Edinburgh, who had been Padre to the 4th Battalion for several years before he became the Radio Padre during the war, and the Reverend Hugh Mackay, the minister of Duns, who for many years was Chaplain to the KOSB Battalion of the Army Cadet Force. With his encouragement the stand of colours of the 1st Battalion is now laid up in the kirk at Duns.

Dumfries: 7 March 1973

By this time the 1st Battalion had returned from Korea after a highly successful operational tour, during which the Battalion earned no fewer than thirty decorations, including the Victoria Cross (to Private Speakman), four Distinguished Service Orders, five Military Crosses, four Distinguished Conduct Medals and sixteen Military Medals. This last medal was highly prized by the soldiers and it was foolishly withdrawn twenty years later – in the interests of 'equality'. I've never met a single soldier who agreed with the Government decision. Another case of political correctness. The Commanding Officers in Korea were Lieutenant Colonel John Macdonald and Lieutenant Colonel Denis Tadman. On their return the 1st Battalion were stationed in Ballykinlar, the first of many tours in the province of Northern Ireland over the next half-century.

Both the Territorial Army Battalions had been re-formed fairly soon after the war, the 4th Battalion under Lieutenant Colonel Harcourt Rae and the 5th Battalion under Lieutenant Colonel Walter Ross who, as a Gunner officer, had given valuable fire support from his 25-pounder guns to the 4th Battalion during the war.

The Freedom ceremony was held on the Whitesands, a broad 'parade ground', hard by the River Nith, which fortunately was in benevolent mood, because the Whitesands from time to time are flooded. All four Battalions of the Regiment were on parade and a large crowd awaited the arrival of Princess Alice, the Colonel-in-Chief. The Freedom scroll was presented to Her Royal Highness by Provost Tom Bell, who later took the salute in a march past in Irish Street. The Provost and magistrates later entertained Her Royal Highness in the Station Hotel and the officers and soldiers were similarly entertained in the County Hotel and the Imperial Restaurant.

This was the first Freedom in the western half of the Regimental area and a very fitting tribute to the many 'Doon Hamers' who had served with the KOSB for generations. (Why 'Doon Hamers'? When men from Dumfries were stationed away from their home territory they invariably said they were 'going doon hame' for the weekend.)

Kelso: 18 April 1973

When Her Royal Highness Princess Alice accepted the Freedom of Kelso from Provost James Stewart, she said, 'It is always a pleasure to return to the land of my birth. It is a particular pleasure to be here in this lovely market place of Kelso for this historic ceremony.' How true! With the backdrop of its beautiful Town Hall and a feast of flowerbeds all round the square, it was a memorable setting for a Freedom ceremony as the Pipes and Drums and Guard of Honour swung into the square. Guarding the colours were Lieutenant Andy Middlemiss and 2nd Lieutenant Hope with Company Sergeant Major Cameron and Sergeants Craig and Wood (later Lieutenant Colonel George Wood, Assistant Regimental Secretary), who came from Ayton.

In his address Provost James Stewart welcomed the Duchess of Gloucester as 'a Borderer, a Scott of Buccleuch, whose family has provided great service to the county of Roxburghshire and to Scotland'. Her Royal Highness, in reply, stressed what a pleasure it was to be in this lovely square; the granting of the Freedom would strengthen the bonds between the burgh and the Regiment and it was abundantly clear that the honour was a unanimous expression of the town's regard. Her Royal Highness also said: 'Far too often young men have been taken from these peaceful counties and many have paid the supreme sacrifice.'

Her words were certainly borne out by the large number of Kelso Laddies who had distinguished themselves in the Second World War: Colonel Donald Hogg MC of Kersmains, Major Allan Innes of Windywalls, and Lieutenant Colonel Jamie Stormonth-Darling MC, later distinguished Chief Executive of the National Trust for Scotland. In the Korean War Sir William Purves had won the Distinguished Service Order Medal for outstanding bravery at the age of nineteen, and Major Alastair Brooks the Military Cross.

Kelso were extremely generous hosts to 192 guests.

Selkirk: 10 October 1973

There was no town in the Borders which provided, per head of population, more volunteers for the KOSB than Selkirk – except perhaps for Newcastleton (invariably known as 'Copshawhame') in the hills near Langholm. Sir Walter Scott, 'the Shirra', himself a Territorial soldier, whose statue stands in front of the courthouse in Selkirk, would have been 'gey prood' as the representatives of all four serving Battalions of the KOSB received the Freedom of the Ancient Royal Burgh in Victoria Park on the banks of the Ettrick from Provost Alexander Macdonald. Thousands of 'Souters' watched the ceremony. The detachment from the 1st Battalion was commanded by Lieutenant Allan Cameron with Company Sergeant Major Ritchie and Sergeants Fleming and Castles and the colours were escorted by 2nd Lieutenants Sandy Rundell and Bob Riddle with Company Sergeant Major 'Busty' Murdoch and Sergeants Laing and Keats. Lieutenant Colonels Turner Dundas and Harcourt Rae and the Roberts were only three of the many KOSB families from Selkirk who were thrilled to see the Regiment honour their ancient burgh.

A unique feature of the Selkirk Freedom was provided by

the Colonel-in-Chief, the Duchess of Gloucester, who followed her father, the Duke of Buccleuch, by 'licking the birse'. This traditional oath of fealty had been carried out by her father in 1932 when he was made a burgess of the burgh. It signifies the ancient craft of shoemaking. The birse is a bristle attached to the end of a shoemaker's waxed thread.

Among the distinguished guests at Selkirk were Major General 'Tiger' Miles, Colonel of the Regiment, the Duke and Duchess of Buccleuch, the Earl and Countess of Dalkeith, Sir Samuel Strang Steel, Lord Lieutenant of Selkirkshire, and Lieutenant General Sir Colin ('Tiny') Barber, General Officer Commanding-in-Chief of Scottish Command.

Stranraer: 11 October 1973

For all concerned, and particularly the writer, who had to organise the whole thing from an office desk at the HQ of the 5th Battalion in Dumfries, two Freedom Ceremonies in the Borders in one weekend, over 100 miles apart, were a real headache. As usual 'the Terriers' came up trumps and transport and accommodation problems were overcome 'somehow'. Her Royal Highness the Duchess of Gloucester, the Colonel-in-Chief, was just as hassled as everyone else as she had to move from her brother's home at Bowhill to Lady Stair's gracious home at Lochinch.

The *Borderers Chronicle*, the Regimental magazine of the KOSB, recorded that: 'The streets were gay with bunting and thronged with people. Bright sunshine glinted on the bayonets of the troops as they formed three sides of a square in Stair Park.'

In her speech Her Royal Highness recalled with very sincere sympathy the lives which had recently been lost in a ferry disaster on the Stranraer to Larne crossing. Her Royal Highness also made mention of the fact that Wigtownshire had at one time owed allegiance to another Regiment (the Royal Scots Fusiliers, based in nearby Ayrshire), but, despite the long distance across the Border to Berwick, Galloway had remained staunchly loyal to the KOSB in two World Wars, and the 7th (Galloway) Battalion had fought magnificently at the Battle of Arnhem in 1944, with a great loss of life and many taken as prisoners of war.

After the parade the troops marched through the town 'with bayonets fixed, drums beating and colours flying'. Provost Dyer took the salute and the local paper reported that he did so 'amid a great press of people'.

Local 'worthies' who were particularly proud that day were the Hannay brothers, who had given splendid service to the 5th Battalion in the Second World War.

There was an intriguing postscript to the Stranraer Freedom: although the ceremony was held on 11 October, the Freedom scroll held at RHQ is dated 10 October! What do people say about 'Everything west of the River Cree?'

Melrose: 25 July 1974

'Impressive Scenes at Ceremony in Historic Old Abbey' was the headline in the *Southern Reporter*'s account of the granting of the Freedom of Melrose to the KOSB. The Duchess of Gloucester, who was to receive the Freedom scroll from Provost John Frater, was no stranger to Melrose for she had spent her early life and holidays at nearby Bowhill and Eildon Hall, with its glorious view of the beautiful Eildon Hills. Her lifelong friend and lady-in-waiting, Dame Jean Maxwell-Scott of nearby Abbotsford, was very well known in Melrose. Only the weather spoiled an outstanding Regimental occasion, but luckily the rain held off for the actual Freedom ceremony in the superb surroundings of the damaged but proud Melrose Abbey. The introductory prayer was given by the Reverend Bob Henderson, the minister of Melrose, who, as a young serving officer in the Black Watch, had been awarded the Distinguished Service Order at the crossing of the River Rhine in 1945. The Freedom scroll was read by the Town Clerk Mr Frank Smart, who was better known in the Regiment as Captain Frank Smart, a most efficient staff officer in the 155th Lowland Infantry Brigade in the Second World War, in which the 4th Battalion KOSB served. The names in Melrose, particularly in the rugby team, are all very well known, and it was most appropriate that Provost John Frater, one of the most familiar names, should have the honour of presenting the Freedom scroll to Her Royal Highness. After the march past, Her Royal Highness met a good number of ex-servicemen at the location which is dear to the heart of all Melrosians, the famous Greenyards rugby ground. Perhaps the proudest to be presented were the author's brother, Ben, who was gravely wounded at Tobruk, and his erstwhile second-row partner in the Melrose rugby team, Bob Cowe of the 6th Battalion KOSB.

Wigtown: 27 July 1974

The county town of Wigtown was honoured by the presence of Her Royal Highness, Princess Alice, the Duchess of Gloucester to grant the Freedom of Burgh. Her Royal Highness was accompanied by the Earl of Stair, the Lord Lieutenant of Wigtownshire. Provost John McColm welcomed the Regiment to the town. In his speech conferring the Freedom the Provost reminded the large audience that Wigtown had sent its citizens to the KOSB in both World Wars and one of them, Colour Sergeant McGuffie, had been awarded the Victoria Cross for conspicuous gallantry in the First World War. The senior officer in the Regiment locally was Major 'Teedo' Stevens, the local Headmaster and the Second-in-Command of the 5th Battalion KOSB. Another local Regimental Borderer, Major Ian Drape, the Provost of Whithorn, was anxious to give the freedom of his burgh to his beloved Regiment, but time would not permit. However amends were made some years later when a commemorative plaque was unveiled outside the old Town Hall of Whithorn.

Newton Stewart: 29 July 1974

Provost Deacon, in welcoming the Regiment to Newton Stewart, said that this was the first Freedom Newton Stewart had ever granted. The Regiment was represented by a Colour Party and a Guard of Honour provided by A Company of the 1st Battalion under the command of Major Colin Mattingley, with the Pipes and Drums and Military Band. I accepted the Freedom scroll on behalf of the Colonel-in-Chief and, in my acceptance speech, I said, 'The men who lived by the banks of the Rivers Cree, Bladnoch and Tarff had never hesitated to come forward in defence of their country. The names on the local war memorials tell their own story.' The Provost made a generous donation to the welfare funds of the Regiment.

Kirkcudbright: 30 July 1974

The Harbour Square in Kirkcudbright was a fine setting for the Freedom of the Royal Burgh, renowned for its association with artists and the Solway fishing trade. The KOSB Territorials always had a strong detachment, not least because the post-war Commanding Officer, Lieutenant Colonel Walter Ross, farmed nearby. There was also a close association with the staff at the Royal Armoured Corps Ranges which were used by the Infantry as a training area.

Provost Dr Dick Rutherford inspected the Guard of Honour which was provided by A Company of the 1st Battalion under the command of Major Colin Mattingley. The key appointments were held as follows: Colour Party, 2nd Lieutenant John Kirkwood and Lieutenant Alastair Cunningham; ensigns, Warrant Officer Class 2 Ted Blythe, Sergeant Andy Ross and Sergeant Fred Noon; stick orderlies, Lieutenant Corporal Frank Currie and Private William Charczuk.

This Guard of Honour became very expert at Freedoms as they provided the Guard for no fewer than six Freedom ceremonies in a row: Melrose, Wigtown, Newton Stewart,

Kirkcudbright, Hawick and Coldstream. As they had come from Berlin via Belfast, it was a fairly hectic time, and they acquitted themselves superbly.

Hawick: 1 August 1974

Of all the Border towns Hawick undoubtedly has the greatest sense of history and tradition. Although the Borders had been ravaged by invaders for centuries, Hawick has been recorded in story, song and tradition more than any of the other Border burghs. Proudly they sing 'Hawick's Queen o' a' the Borders'. Like all the other towns it has sent its proud young Teris off to war. 'Teri' is derived from the war-cry 'Tyr e Bus y Teriodin', ('Nordic Gods of war, sons of heroes slain at Flodden'). It was, therefore, only to be expected that Provost David Atkinson and the Town Council would wish to honour their local Regiment and they chose the most propitious date – 1 August, also commemorating the Regiment's most treasured battle honour, Minden 1759.

The parade took place on the large Common Haugh 'where Slitrig dances doon the glen tae meet the Teviot water'. Over 150 of the Regiment were on parade under the command of Major Colin Mattingley. Provost Atkinson welcomed all ranks of the Regiment and the honoured guests, who included several Provosts from the other Border towns, David Steel MP, and Chay Blyth, the transatlantic rower, who had received the Freedom of Hawick himself not long before.

Since it was Minden Day, the traditional roses were presented to everyone on parade by the Provost. Unfortunately, although the weather was fine, it was very windy and many roses lay at the roadside during the march past which followed. The Town Clerk, Mr William Hogg, read out the 'Burgess Ticket', a long document conferring the Freedom and extolling the virtues of the King's Own Scottish Borderers. The Provost added his praise and, in accepting the scroll, I referred to the generations of 'Teris' who had served the Regiment, many of them paying the supreme sacrifice. I also thanked the people of Hawick for the hospitality they had shown to the thousands of soldiers who had been stationed at nearby Stobs camp over the years.

Taking the salute at the Town Hall, the Provost was flanked by his two halberdiers, who were former members of the Regiment, Messrs William Allan and James Anderson. The local newspaper recorded that the 'crowds stood four deep in the High Street watching the spectacle.'

The biggest cheer went to the large body of ex-servicemen who paraded behind the troops under the command of Lieutenant Colonel J. B. Marshall, a kenspeckle figure with flowing moustaches. Other prominent ex-servicemen were three veterans from the First World War who had fought at Gallipoli and in Palestine, Lieutenant Colonel Jimmy Scott-Noble, who had been an outstanding staff officer with the Highland Division in the Second World War, and Major John Aitkin, who had served after the war in Malaya.

Coldstream: 3 August 1974

The Freedom of Coldstream to the KOSB was unique in the Borderland in that it was the second Regiment to be so honoured by the Royal Burgh, for the Coldstream Guards had, of course, been awarded the Freedom some years earlier.

The Colonel-in-Chief was unfortunately unable to accept the honour personally and she kindly invited the Colonel of the Regiment, Brigadier Frank Coutts, to accept the honour on her behalf. This was a happy decision for the Colonel because his father had been minister of the Rodger Memorial Church in Coldstream half a century before and was still remembered by some of the older citizens.

Provost David Lloyd referred to the fact that Coldstream now had the honour of granting their Freedom to two famous Regiments of the Line, Her Majesty's Coldstream Guards and the King's Own Scottish Borderers. The burgh was justifiably proud of its record in providing soldiers for both Regiments. In the case of the KOSB, the common family had provided volunteers in every generation, including one on parade that day, as an Ensign to the Colours.

Jedburgh: 14 May 1975

The Freedom of 'Jethart' was granted to the KOSB on the coldest May day in memory, but a very warm welcome was extended by Provost Gideon Yellowlees and the Town Council of the ancient royal burgh which had provided many fine officers and men to the Regiment. Two families in particular played prominent roles in the Regiment's recent history: Colonel 'Pondo' Jackson of Glendouglas had been a distinguished officer in the First World War and his son, Allan, in the Second. His grandson, 2nd Lieutenant (now Brigadier) Andrew Jackson, was carrying the Regimental Colour at the Freedom Parade and his eldest son, the fourth generation, was planning to join the Regiment. The Sturrock family, father and son, whose lawyers' office overlooked the parade, have been Honorary Legal Advisors to the KOSB for most of the twentieth century. One couldn't forget three superb characters in the 4th Battalion: Tam Dryburgh DCM, whose one-man enactment of the Jedburgh Riding of the Marches crossing the River Jed entertained many a Sergeants' Mess night; Sergeant 'Yokker' Gray, a plumber exuding dry wit; and Charlie McDonald, the first standard-bearer at the Jedburgh Common Riding, trumpet player, brave stretcher-bearer in the front line, and Scottish Rugby internationalist.

Sanquhar: 15 May 1975

The three towns on the upper reaches of the River Nith, Thornhill, Sanquhar and Kirkconnel, were the TA centres for D Company of the 5th (Dumfries and Galloway) Battalion of

The Coutts Family at St Aidan's Manse, Melrose, c. 1938
Back row, left to right: me, Ben, Dad, Mum, Bobby and Wol
Front row, left to right: Maisie, the artist, and Pip

Mum and Dad, Jack and Rose Coutts

A great team – my daughters Fiona (left)
and Sheena

Philip Coutts MBE – the last Fettesian to wear a top hat?

Ben Coutts – 'a legend in his time'

Bobby (right) and I are hiking in Northern Ireland long before The Troubles

Sir Walter Coutts on the occasion of Uganda being granted independence

St Luke's UF Church in Milngavie where Dad was minister from 1921 to 1935 – a smart vacancy committee car awaits (photo courtesy of Alastair Richmond)

St Columba's (Church of Scotland) Church, London which was destroyed in the Blitz in 1942

St Columba's rose again in a more simple architectural style

HRH the Duchess of Gloucester, Colonel-in-Chief of the King's Own Scottish Borderers, inspects the Guard of Honour at one of the sixteen Freedom ceremonies. The Guard Commander is Major Colin Mattingley, later Brigadier Mattingley and Colonel of the Regiment

HRH the Duchess of Gloucester leaving the Canongate Kirk with the Very Reverend Dr Ronald Selby Wright after the laying-up of two battalions of KOSB colours

'Uncle Beach', Flushing, Holland – the KOSB landed here under heavy fire on 1 November 1944

Alan Herriot's brilliant statuette of a Dutch girl saying thank you to a Scottish soldier (photo courtesy Alan Herriot, sculptor)

The Caledonian Canal (photo courtesy of British Waterways Scotland)

Crinan Basin, the gateway to the Atlantic (photo courtesy of British Waterways Scotland)

Neptune's Staircase on the Caledonian Canal – this series of locks is one of Thomas Telford's civil engineering masterpieces (photo courtesy of British Waterways Scotland)

The Avon Viaduct – an impressive 275 metres long and 26 metres high and boasting twenty-three arches, this is the largest structure on the Union Canal (photo courtesy of British Waterways Scotland)

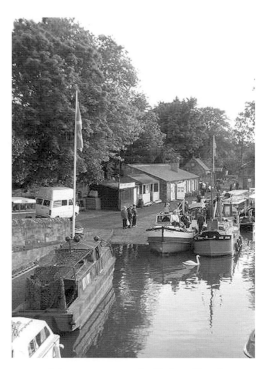

A busy scene on the Union Canal (photo courtesy of British Waterways Scotland)

Colonel Donald Ogilvie Hogg – the daddy of them a'

the Regiment, and the Freedom was a tribute to them. Mainly a farming and mining community, they had provided more than their fair share of soldiers for the Regiment in both World Wars and since.

The ceremony in Sanquhar was unique in that it was the last possible day when any burgh could grant its Freedom because the next day regionalisation was to take place and all the burghs would be incorporated within community councils. The *Dumfries and Galloway Standard* reported that 'it might have been an occasion of sadness at the passing of an era, but instead there was rejoicing that the Council had seen fit to bestow its greatest honour on a Regiment which had such a fine record of service.'

This was an 'inside' ceremony, in St Bride's Church. When Provost James Young was piped to the kirk, the Regiment were delighted to see that he was accompanied by the Lord Lieutenant for Dumfriesshire, Lieutenant General Sir William Turner, the previous and very popular Colonel of the Regiment and General Officer Commanding-in-Chief of Scottish Command. The Freedom scroll was read by Mr William Forsyth, Town Clerk.

After the formal speeches, the troops paraded in Queensberry Square under the command of Major Adam Stavert. After a wreath had been laid at the War Memorial, I read a message from the Colonel-in-Chief to the large crowd and then the parade marched through the town 'with bayonets fixed, drums beating and colours flying'.

The march past entailed the closure of the main road from Dumfries to Glasgow for about half an hour. The Assistant Regimental Secretary explained this somewhat apologetically to the Police Inspector, who immediately responded, 'Nae bother. It'll no' happen again for another 100 years'! Those were the days.

After the Border Burghs had been overtaken by the two Districts with headquarters in St Boswells for the East Borders and Dumfries for the West, Freedoms of the Districts were granted at Galashiels on 5 July 1986, Annan on 22 April 1989, Hawick on 3 June 1989 and Lauder on 14 June 1989.

It is one's hope that these special relationships with the Borders will be honoured from time to time by the new 1st Battalion of the Royal Regiment of Scotland.

Postscript

Berlin: Parade in the Deutschlandhalle for New Colours, 28 February 1974

It is not very far from the truth to say that the Regiment also received the Freedom of Berlin! At the end of its second tour there in 1974 both the townships of Spandau and Charlottenburg invited the 1st Battalion to march through their towns to show their appreciation of the 'best battalion we have had during the occupation of Berlin by the Allied forces'. Large crowds turned out, mainly I suppose because the Berliners are fond of military parades. It was a genuine tribute to Lieutenant Colonel Allan Alstead and his men.

Another historic occasion took place in Berlin when Her Royal Highness the Duchess of Gloucester as Colonel-in-Chief presented new colours to the 1st Battalion in the huge Deutschlandhalle, the location for many important events during Hitler's infamous reign.

Her Royal Highness arrived in a Land Rover, clinging on tightly, before she alighted to inspect the Battalion and present the new colours. It was one of the most spectacular parades in the life of the Regiment.

An opportunity was taken to involve the Regimental area in the week's events and invitations were accepted by Baillie F. Scott of Hawick, Mr W. Main, Town Clerk of Coldstream, Provost Gideon Yellowlees of Jedburgh, Captain Frank Smart of

Melrose, Baillie Mrs Steven, Kirkcudbright, Provost Len Thomson of Selkirk, Provost John Frater of Melrose, Provost Ian Drape of Whithorn, Provost Mrs Murray of Stranraer, the Burgh of Galashiels (whose colours were carried on the town's behalf by an officer), Provost Tom Lennie of Duns, and Provost Jim Stewart of Kelso. At a colourful ceremony in Brooke Barracks, all the burghs who had granted their Freedom to the KOSB presented pipe banners embroidered with the burgh coats of arms to the Regiment, and these are now worn proudly when the Regiment visits each town. It is rumoured that the Berlin nightclubs did unusually good business that week!

That seems to be a fitting note on which to close this short tribute to the King's Own Scottish Borderers, 1689–2006 . . . except to say that before Mr Geoffrey Hoon MP condemned the KOSB to oblivion I hope that one of his aides passed a note to him listing the number of young Borderers who had given their lives for their country during the twentieth century. It makes grim reading:

Campaign	KOSB killed	KOSB wounded
Boer War	111	112
First World War	6,861	22,500
Second World War	1,356	3,250
Korea	70	228
Other conflicts	17	170
TOTAL	8,415	26,260

We Will Remember Them.

Wreath laying at the 52nd (Lowland) Division war memorial in Flushing, Holland,
honouring the fallen during the re-occupation of the Island of Walcheren 1–8 November 1944
(photo courtesy Edith McLean)

Chapter 9

THE DUTCH CONNECTION

Of all the European countries, the Scots undoubtedly hit it off best with the Norwegians, the Danes and the Dutch. I have had close ties with all three. I served for a year with the British Army Training team in Denmark (with the 7th Regiment in Fredericia) and got to know the young men who were called up to reform the Danish Army in 1945–46. Despite the hardships of war they were keen and fit. The call-up period was only six months and a ridiculous rule caused those who were promoted to Kornet (Corporal) to stay on for another three months. Naturally there was not much incentive to develop leadership!

My ties with Norway were more permanent. We had two splendid Norwegian Liaison Officers in the Battalion during the war, Ebbe Roede and Lars Jendemsjo and we naturally got to know them very well. Jendemsjo was too much of a mouthful for the soldiers so, since he was the ski instructor, they just called him 'Jimmy Sna'. After the war we visited them frequently in Bergen and Oslo and got to know their lovely country well. I admire them for everything except the ludicrous price of drinks – most uncivilised. And yet I saw more drunks in Stavanger than I'd ever seen in Edinburgh. Politically I admire them for staying out of the despotic European Union.

Links with Holland started before the Second World War. There was a lot of trade between Holland and Scotland (mainly Dundee) and one of my wife Morag's great-uncles had lived in Veere (Walcheren), where there are still Scots Huises and a former Scots kirk. His kids, invariably wearing the kilt, were stoned in the street during the Boer War. Now Veere is a very upmarket holiday resort with yachts at anchor costing a pretty guilder or two.

In her gap year Morag went to a finishing school at Tilloshena in Switzerland where she met Pam Blandford and Ann McRea, and the three became friends for life. When war broke out, each joined a different service, Pam the RAF, Ann the Army and 'Mog', as they nicknamed her, the Royal Navy.

Morag tragically lost her fiancé, Captain Graham Slinn MC and bar, who was killed in his tank at the crucial battle of Knightsbridge in North Africa while serving in the Royal Nottinghamshire Hussars. Post-war she returned to Tilloshena as an assistant mistress. There she met up with a Dutch girl, Naomi Dudok van Heel who had suffered under the Germans. Her home was at Naarden near Amsterdam on the banks of what was then known as the Zuider Zee, now the Ijsselmer. Morag visited the family there and fell in love with Noami's parents, Harald and Babs Dudok van Heel, a very well-known family in Holland. Harald ('The Colonel') went underground for the whole of the war and the family's hatred for the Germans remains massive to this day. As a result of her war experiences, Naomi suffered a nervous condition. She came more than once to Scotland but she never recovered and died in 1988 after a rather sad life in a mental home. Her parents were a lovely couple and we visited as often as we could, sometimes on our way to Germany. Their son Joris joined the Dutch Navy in London immediately after liberation and had a brief affair with my wife in Bramley, Surrey!

We always hoped that 'The Colonel' would tell us about his dangerous experiences and his part in the war but he was always reluctant to talk about it. Morag managed to persuade Babs to disclose that her husband had been away from home for long periods, a wanted man and always in fear of arrest. On one occasion she was instructed by a member of the Resistance to catch a train at a certain time at a certain station. She entered the carriage to find a tramp sitting opposite her in a totally unkempt condition. It was her husband and this was the only way they could meet.

Only recently, accompanied by my two daughters and a son-in-law, we dined with the van Heels at their delightful home in the woods at Valkeveenselaan in Naarden. Suitably primed by some of his own delicious wine, Joris told us just a little of their occupation by the Germans from 1940 until liberation by the Canadians in 1945 and the 7th Armoured Division (The Desert Rats). Initially, he said, the Germans tried to make friends with the Dutch but the more they tried the more they were disliked. Joris put it like this: 'We soon began to realise that their standards were totally different from ours. The things they admired we hated, and vice versa. It was such a relief to get to England and live in a sane world again.'

In 1943 the Germans' policy changed completely – Anne Frank's universally known book tells it all. Those who failed to comply were packed off to concentration camps in Germany and very many died. Men of eligible age were forced to join up. Joris has previously done his National Service and, at the age of twenty, he was particularly at risk. He decided to lie low. On one occasion he was directed by the Germans to buy a return ticket to a station in the north of Holland. On the train were many young men of the same age and he smelt a rat. He got off the train and returned to Naarden and it probably saved his life. The others who fell for the German ruse were carted off to Germany.

He then told his mother that he must go underground and join the Resistance. Friends told him he would have to be interviewed in secret by the leader of their local No 9 Resistance group. After various preliminary interviews he was shepherded into the great man's presence to be confronted by none other than his own father! He was duly enlisted and became Resistance leader in the Naarden district until the liberation.

Joris's charming wife Agnes had an equally dangerous war. She was eleven years old and lived with her parents in a large farmhouse near Arnhem. Her father played host to many Allied pilots who had been shot down and were on the run. She was never allowed to know their names and was told just to call them 'uncle'. Not surprisingly she said she never knew she had so many uncles – no fewer than forty-four 'uncles' visited them. But the story has an unhappy ending. The Germans caught up with her father and he was sent east like so many others and remained in various concentration camps until finally being liberated by the Americans.

It is good to know that our Dutch friends are as fond of Scotland as we are of Holland. The attraction here is – golf! Our friends come regularly to North Berwick and enjoy the unique quality of the 'gowf' on the many world-noted courses in East Lothian.

Little did I think when I stepped ashore at Flushing in Walcheren in November 1944 that I would marry a girl who had such close connections with Holland. But many a mile had to be trudged and many a river crossed before we reached that happy event in July 1948.

The connections between my Regiment, the King's Own Scottish Borderers, and the towns of Flushing and Middelburg in Walcheren were to become very close. It all started when the fighting was still taking place. Two Battalions of the KOSB were part of the Infantry Brigade detailed to capture the town by assault, landing at Uncle Beach. Not long after the 4th Battalion was ashore, a young man just fifteen years old ventured out of his *keller* (cellar) and bravely ran towards the British lines, asking to see the Commanding Officer. He was Lieutenant Colonel Chris Melville, a Black Watch officer who had played rugby for Scotland. He had Border family connections and was hugely popular with the officers and soldiers of 4 KOSB. The boy was Hans Tuynman and he was welcomed into the Headquarters because he said he knew exactly where the German strong points were. Thereby, he undoubtedly saved lives of KOSB soldiers. Thanks to Hans, the friendship with the good burghers of Vlissingen (Flushing) and Middelburg has flourished for over sixty years. The friendships made between Scots families and their Dutch hosts have now extended to the third and fourth generation. Fortunately it is a two-way traffic and the 4th Battalion Reunion in Hawick would never have been the same without our friends from Walcheren. One special relationship developed: Jack Webster, the eminent newspaper correspondent and author from Maud in Aberdeenshire – where as a boy he had befriended the 4th Battalion KOSB – discovered that he was the same age as Hans Tuynman and so a bond developed between them, broken only by Mr Tuynman's death in 2005. We will always remember his cheery smile as he swung in his wheelchair to the front of the church in Flushing for the 60th anniversary thanksgiving for the liberation.

After the war, the man who fostered this remarkable relationship was a Private soldier in 4th Battalion KOSB, one Gideon Lumsden from Hawick, a member of the Signals Platoon. The Signals Platoon was composed of Jocks who had more than average intelligence and were capable of manning the incredibly poor signals equipment with which the British Army was equipped in those days. (I trust that they are better now.) At a Platoon meeting in Belgium before the 4th Battalion broke up in 1946, Gid was the unlikely choice to be Honorary Secretary of the post-war Signals Platoon Reunion. He carried out this task with such aplomb that the reunion, despite his sad death in 1995, is still flourishing sixty years later.

Enter at this stage a remarkable character, Gid Lumsden's daughter, Frances Paxton, also from Hawick, who has provided the author with the gripping story of the development of the link between Walcheren and the Borders of Scotland. Her father started reunions of the Signals Platoon in the late 1940s, first in Edinburgh, then occasionally in Galashiels, but most support came from Hawick and so it has remained, not just for the Signals Platoon but for continuing reunions for all members of that fine Battalion, the 4th (Border) Battalion KOSB.

No doubt prodded by the membership, Gid Lumsden decided to make contact with the civic authorities in Flushing in 1954, ten years after the liberation of the city, to ask if they would lay a wreath on 1 November on behalf of the 4th Battalion Old Comrades to commemorate the landing. Thus began a permanent relationship with Flushing, first under Burgomaster Kopff and then Bill Poppe, who became a great friend of the Lumsdens and the Regiment and had been a prominent member of the Resistance. From this visit the relationships swelled and new names were constantly being added to our Christmas card list – Adri van Wygen, Bill Peters, the Fastenaus, who used to holiday in Scotland with their caravan in my sister's patch near Dunkeld, and many others when the Inter Scaldis Pipe Band was formed, of which more below.

Two years later, in 1956, Gid and ten members of the 4th Battalion visited Flushing and received a warm welcome, especially from Bill Poppe, at his home and at work in his cheese shop. This was the beginning of many, many thoroughly enjoyable visits to Flushing, particularly on the anniversaries of the original landings in 1944. Sometimes 'higher authority' took over and the senior officers of the 52nd Division came to celebrate the anniversaries and representatives from the other Regiments, the Royal Scots, the Royal Scots Fusiliers, the Cameronians and the Highland Light Infantry and Glasgow Highlanders. On special anniversaries, the Dutch Royal Family would grace the ceremonies.

I can't remember the year – but my Dutch friends assure me

it was in 1983, nearly forty years after our landings at Flushing – that Mr Gaston Timmerman, director of a primary school and a prominent citizen of Flushing, came to visit the 4th KOSB veterans who were staying at the Royal Hotel in Badhuis Straat. Mr Timmerman had been fascinated by the veterans' accounts of the battle for Flushing in 1944 (no doubt some of them 'drawing rather a long bow') and he promised us that he would give the veterans a 'living monument' by starting a traditional Scottish Pipe Band. The band would be established in honour of the 4th KOSB veterans. Gaston was a man of his word and on 23 November 1983 a long article in the local newspaper, the *Provinciale Zeewse Courant,* announced the formation of the Inter Scaldis ('Between the Scheldt') Pipes and Drums. The recruiting campaign for pipers and drummers was effective. Unbelievably, no fewer than twenty enthusiasts replied to the advertisement, a committee was formed with Mr Timmerman as Chairman and Treasurer, and Mr Jan Jacons, a Town Councillor, as Secretary and Legal Adviser. Mr Leen Jobse was appointed Piping Instructor. Registration within six months was important and the band was duly registered as Eerste Zeeuwse Doedelzakband Inter Scaldis Pipes and Drums (27 June 1984) – a bit of a mouthful for future Borderers who would play with the band in Scotland. Among the initial enthusiasts there was a former member of the Argyll and Sutherland Highlanders Military Band, a worker in the shipyards, who had approached the author in the Britannia Hotel (which the Royal Scots had burned to the ground in 1944) to persuade me to permit the new band to wear the Leslie tartan of the KOSB. His request was granted by the Earl of Leven, descendant of our founder, and the then Colonel of the Regiment, Lieutenant General Sir William Turner, who had commanded the 5th Battalion KOSB in the assault on Flushing. It was one of the shipyards, N. V. Haven, which generously offered the band their practice hall, free of charge.

Within a year, the band was active under Pipe Major Jobse, with four sets of pipes costing £235 each – probably too much – with name of supplier withheld. The original uniform consisted of the Leslie Hunting Kilt, with blue sweater, white shirt, a brown waistcoat (ugh!) and sporran, white socks (ugh!) and red flashes and a diced Glengarry with KOSB crest (totally unauthorised, FC).

By this time Jim Coltman of Hawick had taken over from Frances Paxton as Honorary Secretary of the 4th Battalion Reunion, and a very energetic and efficient one he has been for the last twenty years. Jim is a piper and was of considerable help in advising the Inter Scaldis about the various bits of kit and uniform they would require and the right sort of firms to use in Scotland. (Author's protest: like most pipe bands the Inter Scaldis had proportionately more drummers than pipers. The drummers are only 'the Pipers' Labourers' and should only introduce a background to the pipe music, never dominate it, as they invariably do in Scotland.) The only kit the band had when they started were four second-hand side drums and two tenor drums. Now they are fully equipped and magnificently turned out.

The sound of the pipes and drums was undoubtedly popular in the town and villages. Engagements came in regularly and helped to swell the funds. Running a pipe band is a very expensive business and the committee were obviously wise in their financial provision. Even an invitation to open a new chip shop was welcome! There was strong financial backing from some members, charity funds helped and another ten uniforms were purchased in 1985.

In 1986 the band entered the big time and started to enter national competitions. Twenty-one engagements were undertaken and the band appeared on television for the first time. On one very special occasion the band played at the ceremonies surrounding the Delta Project on 4 October 1986.

Memories are short and few will remember that a disastrous 1,800 people were drowned in Zeeland when large parts of the province were inundated. By the end of 1987 the band consisted of fifteen pipers and eight drummers. The writer can certify that their musical ability was first-class and they also provided a thoroughly enjoyable social programme with a fine Scottish country dancing item by delightful and skilled dancers.

The Inter Scaldis Pipes and Drums is not just a band but a family of most delightful people. They really are a family, with some families providing two or three members. With strong links with Folkestone (with which Flushing is twinned), they all speak English with a fluency which embarrasses even the most knowledgeable of Scots. They are all utterly charming and a pleasure to meet. Their musical skills are merely an adjunct to their social affability. The leaders at this stage were Pipe Major Leen Jobse, Pipe Sergeant Jan Kooman and Drum Sergeant Leeuw van Weenen.

By this time the relationship between the KOSB and the Inter Scaldis Pipes and Drums was very close and the standard of their music was such that there was no hesitation in inviting them to play with the Regiment when they celebrated their 300th anniversary by marching down Princes Street, Edinburgh. The Nisson Shipping Company very kindly paid the band's expenses. The band took the opportunity to play together with the Pipes and Drums of the 1st Battalion KOSB. This was a fine achievement after only five years of their existence.

That same year Gid Lumsden led a large party of 4th Battalion veterans to celebrate the 45th anniversary of the landings. The band led the 4th Battalion contingent from the Royal Hotel, their usual 'howff' in Flushing.

On 10 September 1991 Marcel Adriaanse took over as Pipe Major and for the next decade the band went from strength to strength. The standard of their playing was put to the test when they entered several competitions and came away with four wins and two third places in Grade 4. Two World Champions from Scotland, Tom Spiers (piping) and Tom Brown (drumming) gave master-classes.

The Inter Scaldis have sealed their relationship with the King's Own Scottish Borderers by crossing the North Sea every summer to attend the Regiment's Minden Day parade at Berwick-upon-Tweed. They were augmented by local pipers from the Borders, like Jim Coltman from Hawick. They gave freely of their time to entertain the spectators before the parade and gave performances in several towns throughout the Borders. They certainly didn't expect to be pampered for they lived in the cadets' barrack accommodation and 'did' for themselves in the very rudimentary kitchen and dining areas.

Although the KOSB is to be merged with the Royal Scots on Minden Day, 1 August 2006, in Edinburgh, Minden Day ceremonies at Berwick-upon-Tweed will surely continue and the Inter Scaldis Pipes and Drums will always be welcome.

Scotland certainly played its fair share, possibly more than its fair share, in the liberation of the Netherlands from German occupation. The three Scottish Divisions were all heavily involved: the 51st (Highland) who had fought all the way from El Alamein, through Sicily, then to Normandy and on – on – on to the heart of Germany; the 15th (Scottish) from Normandy to the Baltic; and the 52nd (Lowland) from Flushing right into East Germany. Every single Scottish Regiment was there: the Royal Scots Greys (in tanks), Scots Guards, the Royal Scots, the Royal Scots Fusiliers, the King's Own Scottish Borderers, the Cameronians (Scottish Rifles), the Highland Light Infantry, the Black Watch, the Seaforth Highlanders, the Queen's Own Cameron Highlanders, the Gordon Highlanders and the Argyll and Sutherland Highlanders. From the Commonwealth came no fewer than seventeen Regiments with

Scottish titles: Black Watch of Canada, Perth Regiment, Highland Light Infantry of Canada, Stormont Dundas and Glengarry Highlanders, New Brunswick Rangers, North Nova Scotia Highlanders, Cape Breton Highlanders, Cameron Highlanders of Canada, Essex Scottish, 48th Highlanders of Canada, Argyll and Sutherland Highlanders of Canada, Lake Superior Regiment, Queen's Own Cameron Highlanders of Canada, Calgary Highlanders, Seaforth Highlanders of Canada, Canadian Scottish Regiment, and Toronto Scottish. *Seventeen Regiments!* More than those of the Scots themselves. Do people realise what an enormous contribution the Canadians made towards the war effort? And still today they are providing detachments for the United Nations in dangerous places, largely unreported in the United Kingdom.

After his retiral from the Army, as General Officer Commanding-in-Chief of Scottish Command, that very far-seeing General, Sir Derek Lang, foresaw the need to commemorate initially the role of the 51st (Highland) Division and later that of all the Scottish Regiments listed. He formed a Trust, named Golden Pheasant after the code name of a Divisional attack on the west side of the River Maas – another golden thread, because the Trust flourished and eventually arranged for the opening of a small Scottish Room in the Dutch War Museum at Overloon. The centrepiece of this room is a beautiful sculpture, depicting a Scottish piper being presented with flowers by a small Dutch girl. A replica of the Scottish Room is also now housed in the Training Centre of Redford Barracks in Colinton Road, Edinburgh. It was beautifully sculpted by Alan Herriot. The Scottish Room was officially opened by General Sir Jeremy Mackenzie in the presence of Lady Lang – for sadly Sir Derek had died before his dream was realised – and a dedicated party of veterans from the Highland Division. Dr Tom Renouf MM, Black Watch, had been a tower of strength in making the arrangements. The Lowland Regiments were very well represented by Mr Donald Fairgrieve, a retired KOSB officer who did an immense amount of work in preparing the artefacts. Like all of us he was hooked by General Derek's charm – you just couldn't say 'No'. The pipers were provided by the ever-willing Inter Scaldis Pipe Band from Flushing. The panels in the display are beautifully presented and tell, very briefly, the total involvement by Scots troops from home and abroad in the liberation of the Netherlands from Nazi occupation.

After the crossing of the Rhine when Holland was fully liberated it was the Canadian Divisions who discovered that the Dutch were starving nearly to death and they set about providing relief quickly. My Canadian cousin, Jock Fleming, whose young brother Bobby had been killed in Normandy, transferred from the 'Sappers' (Engineers) to the Infantry in order to avenge his brother's death, but he found himself instead in Northern Holland dealing with the terrible privations which the retreating Germans had left behind.

Sixty years after the liberation, in 2005, the Netherlands Government very generously decided to offer a commemorative medal to all those who had taken part in the liberation. It is a very colourful medal in the national colours (left to right, red, white and blue), with a touching inscription: 'Thank You Liberators'. For once the British Government, who are rather sensitive about medals, accepted it (how many did Monty receive?) and the Netherlands Consul General in Edinburgh, Mr Michael Hughes, very kindly came down to Hawick to present them to the twenty or so surviving members of the 4th Battalion who had fought their way through Holland to Germany. It was a gesture very much appreciated by the liberators and their families.

The Falkirk Wheel, surely now one of the world's wonders

Chapter 10

A PLAIN MAN'S GUIDE TO THE SCOTTISH CANALS

After my Army service and ten years with British Legion Scotland, I found it difficult to 'retire'. I wouldn't call myself a workaholic but I had an active body and mind and had to be doing something. Nowadays, retired Service officers seek highly paid positions as consultants. In my day the norm was that you offered your administrative experience to a charity or charities without charge – and so it was that I was attracted towards a newly formed trust, the oddly named the Seagull Trust which, as I mentioned in the Preface, provides free canal cruising in Scotland for disabled people. This drew me inevitably towards a close interest in Scotland's Inland Waterways. I spent twenty years with them and saw them grow from one vessel, carrying 482 passengers, to eight well-designed craft giving pleasure to over 13,000 disabled people each year. When the Millennium Link was proposed, a vastly imaginative project costing £78 million, I became deeply interested and started to research the history of our fascinating canals. I have read many books on each of them individually but, as far as I know, this is the first recent description of all four canals which are an important part of Scotland's heritage.

The Scottish public as a whole is abysmally ignorant about its own inland waterways. One of the few positive things which the Scottish Executive of the new devolved Parliament has done is that they have taken an interest in Scotland's canals, the Crinan, the Caledonian, the Forth and Clyde, and the Union.

Fortunately, transport is a devolved subject and the Executive issued a policy document in 2004 entitled *Scotland's Canals: An Asset for the Future.* In the Foreword, Mr Iain Gray MSP, the Minister for Enterprise, Transport and Lifelong Learning, says, *inter alia*: 'We want the people of Scotland to rediscover the canals whether through sailing, walking, cycling or enjoying the varied flora and fauna . . . This paper sets out our aspirations to unlock the benefits the canal system can bring. We want to use it to raise the profile of canals.'

I therefore have no hesitation in helping the Executive make our canals better known to the readers of this book.

They are probably aware of the Caledonian and Crinan Canals because public roads run alongside, but of the Forth and Clyde and Union Canals they know practically nothing, because the canals pass through towns and the countryside, invisible to the casual onlooker. I have spoken to Morningside ladies who have no idea that the Union Canal runs through the delightful Harrison Park and on into the Lochrin basin, adjacent to Lothian Road, right in the heart of the city.

Having mentioned them first, let us deal with the Crinan and the Caledonian.

The Crinan Canal

The great obstacle facing sea-going traffic from the Clyde to the Western Isles was the fearsome passage round the Mull of Kintyre where many a good ship has foundered in the wild conditions – and even in recent times a very powerful helicopter came to grief in very thick fog. A short-cut was vital to the all-important fleet of puffers, the workhorses of the Western Isles, known to many through Neil Munro's hilarious tales of the *Vital Spark*, which plied the waters of the Outer Isles, engendering scenarios which were a positive hoot. The puffers were the life-blood of the Hebrides, carrying the essential coal and other supplies to make life possible on these inhospitable (weather-wise anyway) islands. Long before *Whisky Galore*, the hospitable 'dram' played a large part in the social life of the islands, despite the rigours of the Free Kirk.

The Government decided that something must be done. Supported by the Duke of Argyll, studies were made of two possible routes, one from Tarbert to West Loch Tarbert and one from Loch Gilp through to Loch Crinan. Eminent engineers James Watt and John Rennie, and even the famous Thomas Telford at a later stage, were involved in the selection of the latter route and the completion of the work. The canal would be nine miles long – a huge saving of time and money compared with 'the Mull'. There would be fifteen locks and the highest point of the canal would be 68 feet above sea level. Canals were the 'in' thing in England as the latest and cheapest means of commercial travel and Scotland had to have its share. Parliament approved the canal in 1793 and work started a year later.

As with all canals there were problems – always finance, always almost insurmountable problems with stone on the one hand and bog on the other, and in this case also labour. The environment was very inclement and the workmen (navvies) demanded high wages as compensation. Even the Army in Scotland had to be approached to supply labour – a forerunner of the Military Aid to the Community in force today.

The Crinan Canal was finally opened in 1801. Naturally there were teething problems, the worst of which was the collapse of a reservoir in 1811. The relief of the skippers, under steam let alone sail, who were spared the tempestuous Mull of Kintyre must have been enormous. Traffic slowly increased and really took off when the Caledonian Canal was reopened in 1822. It was possible for shipping to proceed all the way from Glasgow to Inverness, using the two canals. The canal was used not just for commercial vessels, but was extremely popular with passengers, either proceeding to the Western Isles or more popularly for pleasure trips. There are many photographs of happy passengers on the *Linnet*, which carried a full complement.

In 1847 the route received a real 'PR' shot in the arm when that most intrepid of all travellers in the Highlands, Queen Victoria, with Prince Albert, decided to travel to Inverness via the Crinan and the Caledonian. This was, of course, some years before the railways pushed north of the central belt and prior to the ritual of the Monarch arriving in state at Ballater Station. Her Majesty was a little impatient with the delay caused by the canal locks. By that time she perhaps had not become used to the slow pace of life in the Highlands, where there is always time for a 'crack' and a puff at the clay pipe. Nowadays pleasure yachts and tourism justify the very large cost of the Crinan Canal's upkeep. The highlight of the year on the Crinan is the annual Clyde Cruising Club Tobermory Race, when every berth and every lock are full of happy yachtsmen and women bent on the excitement of sailing competitively on the open sea.

No mention of any canal would be complete without the details of the one essential commodity – water, and lots of it. Every time a lock is opened and shut there is a considerable loss of water, which must be replaced. In this case the vital supplies came from seven lochs south of Cairnbaan. When they are at their normal level all is sweetness and light, but when they run low it causes considerable consternation among the local rod fishermen, who enjoy the most popular sport in Scotland – the 'fushin''.

Canals don't come cheap. The income from the users of the Crinan Canal in 2000–01 was £341,000 and the expenditure £1,050,000. After the Millennium Link the income has slightly decreased and the expenditure increased. Good value for a vital waterway and a superb tourist opportunity.

I have not attempted to describe the Crinan Canal itself. Come and see for yourself. It's magic!

The Caledonian Canal

Who would ever have believed in the year 1800 that they could build a canal right through the Highlands of Scotland? Whether it was the pressure of the Navy, who were afraid of being caught out in the Clyde when the enemy, then the French, turned up in the Baltic, or once again the fear of the very wild passage through the Pentland Firth, the Government were determined to go ahead. Between 1803 and 1822 they very cleverly linked up the existing Lochs, Lochy, Oich, Ness (no doubt disturbing the monster), and Dochfour. Very complicated locks were required at various places, especially at Loch Oich, with fifteen locks, and fourteen at Corpach. Nowhere is it more than 106 feet above sea level. The Caledonian Canal is sixty miles long but only twenty-two miles are 'cut'; the rest are natural lochs. It is much broader and deeper than the other canals, clearly designed to take all types of sea-going vessels up to a certain tonnage.

The principal architect was the amazing Thomas Telford, who left his mark on countless bridges, viaducts, aqueducts and many other brilliant architectural achievements through-out Great Britain. It was no wonder that he was elected the first President of the Institute of Civil Engineers.

There are so many extraordinary features about this remarkable canal that it would take up too much space in this humble guide to elaborate upon them. Each section of the canal has its own architectural features which have overcome the difficulties of the environment. The entry from the North Sea at the eastern end of the canal is most imposing. The sea lock is built of huge pieces of red sandstone hewed in the Red-castle quarries on the north side of the Firth. Thereafter, there are a series of locks at Clachnaharry which lead to the large Muirtown basin. This is a fine assembly point for commercial traffic, but nowadays is full to capacity with enormous yachts. The plain man wonders at the enormous cost of these vessels — perhaps a pointer to the economic state of the country. In any case they provide a fine sight when they unfurl their sails and head west for Fort William and the Atlantic.

Muirtown basin is also the home of the *Highland Seagull*, the boat owned by the Seagull Trust, which provides free canal cruising for over 13,000 disabled people in Scotland every year. Caley Marina very kindly give her free berthing and waive the bridge charges. The daily cruises start each day, April to October, from Tomnahurich ('the hill of the yew trees') bridge and sail to Dochfour – not too far, for the parties are mainly elderly folks. They come from as far afield as Skye in the west, Thurso in the north and Peterhead in the east. Everyone connected with the Trust is a volunteer and the skippers have to be very well trained, bearing in mind that quite large vessels are confronted on nearly every trip. Pleasure boats operated by Jacobite Cruises also sail from Tomnahurich.

So much has been written about Loch Ness and the 'monster'. That may be the only thing that some people know about the Caledonian Canal! The village with the onomatopoeic name of Drumnadrochit and its romantic Castle Urquhart, scene of former battles, are magnets for tourists. Dr Johnson and the diarist Boswell passed this way and received their first experience of Highland hospitality when an old crone in a decrepit bothy brought out her precious bottle of whisky and gave them a dram.

It is not difficult to bring to mind the turbulent history of these parts where memories are long and the clan system strong. General Wade, the road builder of the Highlands, took a firm grip after the Battle of Culloden in 1745 and a series of forts were built to keep the rebellious Highlanders in check. The most famous of these is Fort George on a promontory outside Inverness. It is picturesque for visitors but pretty grim for the military occupants, although their accommodation has been modernised to a high standard. It is still occupied by the Army today, but visitors are welcome. Another of these forts was built at our next stop on the Caledonian Canal, Fort Augustus at the west end of Loch Ness. The military fort was replaced in more peaceful times by an abbey, the home of Benedictine monks. It was built as a monastery and housed a famous boys' school from 1889 until 1997. The military atmosphere continued, for the school had a first-class contingent of the Combined Cadet Force, which I had the privilege to inspect more than once.

The five locks which take traffic west to Loch Oich are always surrounded by holidaymakers and sightseers for they are right in the middle of the village. Beyond the locks the canal 'disappears' for five miles, that is, it cannot be seen from the main road or any other vantage point. As a result it is a favourite spot for sighting wildlife of all kinds, particularly birds and red deer. Reaching Loch Oich, one really appreciates the peace of the area, with gorgeous views in every direction. It is an ideal area for walkers. Nearby is the Great Glen Water Park.

Loch Oich is the highest point of the canal. Thereafter craft begin to descend, heading west. From Loch Oich onwards it is all downhill to the open sea at Corpach near Fort William, with a magnificent view of Britain's highest mountain, Ben Nevis. For ex-servicemen there are reminders that this was 'commando country' in the Second World War. Not far from the canal on the hill towards Spean Bridge stands the magnificent Commando Memorial.

The income from vessels using the Caledonian Canal in 2000–01 was £575,000 and the expenditure £2,300,000. Since the Millennium Link both figures have increased.

The Forth and Clyde Canal and the Union Canal
Another reason why the Forth and Clyde and Union Canals are not so well known is that, although the Crinan and Caledonian Canals have always been operational, the Forth and Clyde was only fully operational from 1790 until 1845, when the arrival

of the railways in Scotland reduced its capacity; it survived until halfway through the First World War, when the Admiralty closed the Forth ports to all shipping. The Union Canal, connecting Edinburgh and the Lothians to the Forth and Clyde at Falkirk, only lasted from 1822 until 1845, a woefully short time after such a huge outlay of capital.

Cutting a new canal was obviously a huge undertaking in engineering skill, the determination to push the project through, the purchase of land and, most of all – money. Many people, even canal buffs, would be surprised to know that it was an Admiral, Sir Charles Campbell, who, in 1760, first mooted the idea of a canal link between the Clyde and the Forth. He feared that, if the fleet were anchored in the Clyde, the enemy might approach from the North Sea and his vessels would have to travel 500 miles round the north of Scotland or 900 round the south of England to reach the North Sea, whereas by canal it would be only sixty-five miles. The argument raged for years at the end of the eighteenth century and eventually it was the merchants of Glasgow who insisted that a canal must be built 'to bolster the trade and wealth of Glasgow'.

A start was made in 1768 at the eastern end and by 1773 it had reached Kirkintilloch, the rest of the journey to Glasgow being completed by cart. Two years later the canal reached Stockingfield near Maryhill, in the heart of Glasgow. Trade flourished but the company ran out of money and it took years to complete the journey to Bowling on the Clyde.

The beginnings of the Union Canal were really the story of relations between Edinburgh and Glasgow over the centuries – no love lost! The merchants of Edinburgh were mighty jealous of the success of the Forth and Clyde. They were desperately short of coal. Glasgow had plenty but Edinburgh relied on coal from Alloa, Fife and Newcastle, which was subject to a duty of 3s. 6d. a ton, a very large amount in those days. A canal route to the west was the only answer. Edinburgh had a stroke of luck.

There was naturally a lot of opposition to the cost involved – 'twas ever thus – but to their aid came the opinion of the master engineer of their time, Thomas Telford (from Langholm). He already had a huge reputation as a successful maritime and bridging engineer and he opined that the Union Canal 'is the most perfect navigation between Edinburgh and Glasgow'. It was to be a 'contour' canal following the natural contours of the countryside, thus obviating the need for many aqueducts and viaducts. The doubters were won over and the work started immediately. Working day and night, the 'navigators', mostly Irish workmen who have left their mark on the route to this day, finished the canal by 1822 and it joined the Forth and Clyde by the use (thought ingenious then) of no fewer than eleven locks. They were very costly in time, finance and water. Who could have guessed that nearly 100 years later the locks would be replaced by a Wheel? The locks are commemorated today by a public house named Lock 15.

Rescuing the Central Scotland Canals

The story of the Central Scotland canals is a sad one. Without proper maintenance – and money – they deteriorate, but they wouldn't go away, as some Governments rather hoped. Water comes in on one side from feeder reservoirs and the overflow must go out the other side. Bridges, open to the public, require maintenance and many of the structures along both canals have become 'listed' and must, by law, be suitably preserved.

Some activity remained. From Milngavie, outside Glasgow, we usually went to school by train, but during the General Strike of 1926 my mother, one of the earliest lady drivers, insisted on taking us to school by car, much to our disgust; it was a bullnose Morris with a two-gallon petrol can on the running board, and we returned the salute of the AA men who then saluted every car with an AA badge! When we got to Temple, near Anniesland Cross, the bascule bridge across the canal was up, so some canal traffic must have been running. School picnics, normally on the back of a farm cart to Balmore, were once replaced, to our enormous excitement, by a canal trip on the *Fairie Queen*, the double-decker cruise ship which ran most successfully for many years on the Forth and Clyde.

On the Union, rowing continued at the Craiglockhart boathouse of the Edinburgh University and George Watson's and George Heriot's Schools. Linlithgow was always canal-friendly. Boating continued there under the guidance of the Linlithgow Union Canal Society.

Nevertheless, the state of the canals deteriorated; weeds grew everywhere. They began to silt up, no one respected them and people endlessly flung their shopping trolleys and other detritus into the canals. In 1965 they were officially closed and referred to contemptuously as 'remainder' canals. What an insult to once-proud waterways.

However, men of faith, who always believed in the restoration of the canals, were at hand. The palm for the No. 1 Saviour of the Central Scotland Canals must go to Ronnie Rusack MBE, who was until recently mine host of the Bridge Inn at Ratho in Midlothian. OK Glasgow – I know that Donald Mackinnon and many others in the Forth and Clyde Canal Society were constantly active, but no one had a gleam in the eye to equal that of Ronnie Rusack, supported by a host of other enthusiasts, such as John Hume, Jamie Sime, Gordon Daly – a virtual army of well-wishers.

Ronnie made the first positive move. He purchased the *Pride of the Union*, the first restaurant boat on the Union. Encouraged by its success, he bought a second one and bravely formed the Edinburgh Canal Centre at Ratho. He has now run holiday boats from Edinburgh to Bowling on the Clyde, with stops at hotels en route.

One man of the faith (in every sense) was the Reverend Hugh Mackay, the minister of Torphichen, adjacent to the

Union, where he took the local Sea Scouts for watermanship. It was then that he had the inspired idea of providing canal cruises, free of charge, for disabled people who would have no other means of having a 'day out'. His inspiration led to the formation of the Seagull Trust. It seemed an unfortunate name to some – the seagull is not a very pleasant bird – but the Reverend Hugh wanted to express the freedom of disabled people, freed from the confines of a hospital ward or a special school. Thanks to his enthusiasm and that of many others it flourished.

(One day the phone rang in the Seagull office and a rough voice on the telephone bellowed: 'Is that the Seagull Trust? I've got a pair o' seagulls stuck up the lum here. Will ye come and clear them oot?')

The Trust was formed in 1978 under the chairmanship of Professor John Hume, a Glasgow lecturer, very knowledgeable about canals (and many other things). It flourished under his leadership and the enormous enthusiasm of Hugh Mackay, the first Honorary Secretary. The first 'narrow boat', as they are called, was gifted by a charity in England and named the *St John Crusader* to acknowledge the great support given to the Trust by the Order of St John. The boats are narrow so as to fit through the many narrow locks on the English canals. In 1979, 475 disabled people cruised from the Bridge Inn in Ratho up to the beautiful Almondell Aqueduct, in just over an hour. There they enjoyed their 'piece' along with another disabled party, before doing the return trip. Everyone connected with the Trust is a volunteer. Many of the skippers are ex-Merchant Marine, more used to steering huge oil tankers in the Gulf than crawling at three knots up a Scottish canal!

A fundraising team was formed, mostly ex-servicemen and women, with a former bank manager, the redoubtable Norman Simpson, as Honorary Treasurer. Soon, new boats were being built, on very generous terms, on the Clyde by good friends in the shipping industry. Seagull Trust branches opened in Ratho (two boats, a reception centre and a dry dock), Falkirk (one boat and boathouse, two boats in 2006), Kirkintilloch (two boats and a boathouse), and Inverness (one boat). As I write the Trust owns these seven vessels, which provide free canal cruises for over 11,000 disabled people every year from April till October. Now a holiday boat, the *Marion Seagull*, very kindly presented by the Salvesen family, takes disabled families for a holiday weekend or longer.

All this activity has taken place while the Lowland canals were still in a very poor state of maintenance, but the Seagull cruises and other activities on both canals were at least helping to keep the weeds down and show some sign of returning life. Don't ask Seagull skippers about the revolting job of removing weed from propellers!

Interest in the canals was increasing by the day. What the Lowland canals needed most of all was *money* – and loads of it. In the year 2000–01, the income from the Forth and Clyde Canal was £518,000 and the expenditure £1,475,000.

Help was at hand in the form of the Millennium Link.

Before that exciting event, the reader ought to understand how our canals are administered. Governance is by British Waterways Scotland (BWS), an independent offshoot of British Waterways UK, mainly financed by them although the Scottish Executive voted to provide £8.1 million in 2001, increasing annually.

People would find it hard to appreciate – I for one – just how much administration is required in running a canal system. Quite apart from the creation of new canals, the works required to maintain the existing network are enormous. It is difficult to allot priorities. To my surprise, reservoirs, which supply the essential requirement of water, only account for two per cent of the waterways' administration, followed by weirs and sluices (seven per cent), locks (eight per cent), buildings (nine per cent), tunnels and culverts (ten per cent), jetties and moorings (fifteen per cent), bridges and aqueducts (sixteen per cent) and, not surprisingly, embankments and cuttings (thirty per cent). A figure of 'three per cent other' leaves one wondering. It takes roughly 200 employees to run Scotland's four canals, more in the summer than in the winter.

BWS is also responsible for encouraging all public bodies sponsored by the Executive to work together and support the sustainable development and regeneration of canals and their surrounding areas, and for promoting voluntary sector and community involvement with particular regard to their educational value and their positive impact on the quality of life.

At one time, before the arrival of the railways, the canals carried huge amounts of freight across the central belt of Scotland. Much thought is being given to encouraging manufacturers to use the canals again for freight, particularly for those items which do not need to be delivered 'in a hurry'. But it is developing only slowly. The great mammon, motorways, have taken over the role of freight delivery almost entirely – and gradually clogged up Britain's road system as a result. Perhaps some sound commercial sense will return – to everyone's benefit. BWS have introduced some vessels very similar to the assault boats we used in the war, principally for recreational purposes – but some entrepreneur might see a commercial possibility here.

BWS is busy improving navigation facilities on all Scotland's canals. Pleasure craft naturally require secure moorings, bank-side toilet facilities, shore power, water, launderettes, and, above all, waste disposal.

The Falkirk Wheel, conceived for the Millennium year 2000, is undoubtedly now one of the wonders of the world. It is a fantastic engineering achievement. Its primary purpose was to allow vessels to pass easily from the Union Canal down to the Forth and Clyde Canal and vice versa without the need for locks, but it has become, certainly in its early years, a major tourist attraction for Scotland. Visitors enjoy a 45-minute journey in futuristic specially adapted vessels through a canal tunnel (only the second in Scotland), along a high columned aqueduct and then dropping spectacularly 25 metres off its end within the world's only revolving boatlift.

The Falkirk Wheel was declared open on 24 May 2002 by Her Majesty the Queen. It was a wet day, but it was a brilliant achievement by BWS to get it ready in time, because there had been an equatorial rain storm a week or so before the opening and much of the surrounding greensward had been swept away. After the official opening, visitors poured in, no fewer than a quarter of a million in the rest of that year. In the next year, 2003, it became a major tourist attraction in Scotland and over 450,000 visitors paid to enjoy the Falkirk Wheel Experience. The income ensured that this part of the Millennium Link became the first Millennium Project to 'pay its way' – and so it will continue for it is a fantastic crowd-puller.

It is essential for the Plain Man's Guide to know:

Who thought it all up?

How on earth was the £79 million for the whole Millennium Link raised?

Who built it?

Who Thought It Up?

From start to finish this was a BWS project. Mr George Ballinger, the Chief Engineer of BWS, told me that 'a unique structure was required at the junction of the Forth and Clyde and Union Canals'. The Millennium Commission, set up by Government to celebrate the year 2000, wished to support projects 'which looked back and also forward'. The next consideration was to encourage waterborne visits. The Lowland canals had had no history of pleasure-boat movements for forty years. There had to be a magnet to attract the public.

Well, they certainly got a magnet in the Falkirk Wheel, as the above visitor numbers prove.

'Getting there' was naturally a long process. 'Brainstorming sessions' were held in our Glasgow office – nothing was considered too stupid! Architects from Dundee, the Nicol Russell Studios, were engaged. The 'Wheel' process gradually evolved and was finally approved.

How Was It Paid For?

The petition to the Millennium Commission was drawn up by BWS and flown to London with a small group of canal enthusiasts, including the author as Honorary Piper. There wasn't a pressman in sight when the petition was solemnly handed into the Millennium offices just behind Westminster Abbey to the tune of 'Scotland the Brave' – or was it 'Over the Sea to Pie in the Sky'? *£79 million?* It was surely impossible? A wee boy flung a penny on the pavement for the piper so the fundraising started in earnest.

The achievement of the final sum is too complicated to explain here, but it was encouraging to hear that voluntary sector and canal societies were instrumental in 'stirring it up', including raising a petition and gaining 30,000 signatures in a short space of time.

There were nine Millennium Commissioners. One of them was known to me and I wrote to him to offer congratulations on pulling off a very fine achievement. I was also bold enough to ask if he would care to comment on the approach the Commissioners had to this apparently hare-brained and very costly proposal. He very kindly replied, apropos the Falkirk Wheel and the thirty-three other obstructions on the Lowland canals, that there had not been any vote as such. It helped to have someone in the group who was really passionate for a particular cause and in his case he was passionately in favour of the Wheel and the Millennium Link. 'But it was equally important to have Commissioners acting as Devil's Advocate.' They could usually be brought round to join the majority view. It had to be stressed that the applications for Millennium projects were oversubscribed by ten times the amount of money available. 'The outstanding things that commanded across the board support got through.' At a dinner to honour Lord Glentoran's retirement, the one single example he quoted of the need to consult people on the ground was the Millennium Link, of which the Falkirk Wheel was the major component. 'It was a colossal achievement but it was the achievement of British Waterways Scotland and all of you on the ground – we were all very proud to have assisted in one of the great successes of the celebration.'

Who Built It?

Thanks to an article in the magazine *New Civil Engineer* it is just possible for the layman to grasp the complexities of this huge engineering project. Various interested parties were invited to attend a meeting 'with only a clear head and a blank piece of paper'. The emergent solution was 'a genuine rare example of design integration between architects, steelworkers, designers and engineers of several disciplines, civil, structural and mechanical'.

The most touching example of the innovative mechanism involved was the simple statement by consultant Tony Gee that he had modelled the cog arrangement with Lego borrowed from his eight-year-old daughter, Sarah, quickly proving the technique's effectiveness. 'Sarah was impressed that I could assemble something without instructions,' said the architect. 'But now she wants the parts back to build her helicopter!'

The preferred contractor was a Morrison–Bachy– Soletanche Joint Venture and they appointed Butterley Engineering to design, fabricate and erect the Wheel. For once design by committee paid dividends. There are no structural codes for boatlifts and Senior Engineer Richard Prosser had to source a dozen international guidelines, varying from Norwegian offshore specifications to Germany's ice codes. The impact of thermal and solar movements and the danger of ice all had to be taken into account.

The decision to pre-assemble the various sections on the factory floor paid dividends later, on site. Bolted connections were preferred to welding, but the mind boggles at the numbers involved – 15,000 bolts with 45,000 bolt holes. The tolerance permitted in assembly was only one millimetre.

Moving this huge amount of equipment by road was in itself a major achievement. Three enormous cranes were hired for a week to complete the wheel erection. They were paid off a day early!

As well as the Wheel, Morrison–Bachy–Soletanche had to build a tunnel 168 metres long, a four-span concrete aqueduct, three locks and new stretches of canal totalling two kilometres.

The first new canal tunnel for a century, subcontracted to Spray Concrete, was routed beneath the main Glasgow–Edinburgh railway line and, more critically, the Antonine Wall, once the Roman Empire's northern boundary. Treading warily because of environmental interests, the contractors created no disturbance to either the railway line or the Antonine Wall because the excavation was through sandstone and boulder clay.

Full marks to BWS for their initiative and to British engineering for completing a canal and tourism creation which has been hailed as one of the Wonders of the World.

Scots – and welcome visitors – these canals are yours and they are free. Sail them, walk them, cycle them, and find extraordinary views and wildlife.

The Duchess of Gloucester congratulates Colour Sergeant Harrigan on the award of the
Long Service and Good Conduct Medal

Chapter 11

THESE I HAVE ADMIRED

This is not a name-dropping exercise, but during our lifetimes we meet thousands of people. Most 'pass in the night' but several create a lasting impression and are always easily recalled to mind. One of the most interesting people I met was the Right Honourable Lord Reith of Stonehaven GCVO GBE CB TD, the founder of the BBC. I suppose some people loved him; most people hated him, but nearly everyone respected him. For some unknown reason he took a 'shine' to the Coutts family. Well, I suppose we had some things in common. We were both sons of the manse in Glasgow, we went to the same school, Glasgow Academy, we were both devoted to the church of our forefathers and we had both served in Lowland Scottish Regiments. A Cameronian, he was, let us say, difficult. He was a mighty unpopular man and you only have to read *Wearing Spurs* to discover why. Nationally, he was an extremely key figure of the establishment in London and rarely came back to Scotland but when he did he always got in touch with one member of the family or another. The occasion Morag and I remember best was in 1968 when he was representing the Queen as Lord High Commissioner to the General Assembly of the Church of Scotland. We were invited to one of the formal dinner parties at the Palace of Holyroodhouse. He was a fine host and we thoroughly enjoyed the meal, accompanied by skilled Army pipers (in subsequent years and most harmoniously replaced by civilians from the Royal Scottish Pipers' Society). After dinner we repaired to the drawing room, where everything was totally informal. One of the guests was Yehudi

Menuhin. He sat in a chair with his magic violin and invited us all to name tunes of our choice. What a privilege! During all this Lord Reith was the essence of charm and you would never guess that he had been such a hard taskmaster as a soldier and the Chairman of the BBC. Brother Wally once wrote to him suggesting that he, Sir Walter, would make a very good Governor of the BBC. Not surprisingly, despite his apparent affection for the family, Reith told him to 'get lost'.

Among the generations of the King's Own Scottish Borderers who struck me as commendable were two with whom I did not even serve – the two Jimmies, Jimmy Tranter and Jimmy Swanston. They were utterly dedicated to the KOSB from the cradle to the grave. Tranter was a Souter, which means he came from Selkirk. It must have been a coincidence but the majority of sergeants whom I had the privilege to command in wartime were Souters, such as Jock Beattie, JAF, Scottish Rugby trialist, not to be confused with his namesake from Hawick who won twenty-one caps for Scotland. Souter Jock was eventually commissioned back to his old Battalion, an unusual distinction, and won a fine Military Cross in North-West Europe. Others were Wat Linton ('The Red Beast'), Stoor Richardson, Jock Smith, my first Platoon Sergeant, and Jim Douglas, his successor. The Shirra, Sir Walter Scott, left a fine military tradition behind him in Selkirk.

When one of these splendid Souters was in his fifties he complained to me at a reunion: 'Only get the leg over three times a year now – at the Common Riding, on Auld Year's Nicht and the day the Co-op divi comes in.'

Jimmy Tranter joined the TA before the war and served during the war, as a KOSB, with the outstanding 52nd (Lowland) Reconnaissance Regiment, commanded by the most under-promoted officer in the British Army, Lieutenant Colonel Jack Hankey, who later returned to his pre-war appointment as TA Secretary in Galashiels. He looked after the TA and cadets in the Eastern Borders. Jack should undoubtedly have reached the highest ranks of the British Army – but he kept speaking his mind to senior officers! Tranter was known to everybody as a 'character'. With his chums Tom Moffat and 'Budge' Burgess, he was the life and soul of the Army Cadet Force. At annual camp everyone looked forward to the competition when the three of them put their wallies (false teeth for the uninitiated) into a pint of beer, drained the lot and had to decide whose teeth they had (nearly) drunk. At a Burns Night supper in Berwick he was proposing the Immortal Memory, having partaken liberally, when he came to the critical point where he had to stab the haggis; he took an almighty sweep with his bayonet – and missed by a good eighteen inches! We all thought Willie Swan (Sir William), the Cadet Commandant, would die laughing. After retiral, Tranter looked after the Duke of Buccleuch's car park at Bowhill and was known to hundreds of visitors, whom he would greet by saying anent His Grace: 'Him and me's on Christian name terms.' Jimmy Swanston was of a completely different nature. You can't get more loyal to your Regiment than call your house 'Borderers' Neuk'. He was one of those heroes in the 7th Battalion KOSB, who, against hopeless odds, landed at Arnhem as a Sergeant Major. He lost a leg in action and was taken prisoner, but I have never heard a word of complaint. He just adored the Army life. Still very much with us at the time of writing, he has devoted his life to the welfare and comradeship of his fellow soldiers. You can read more in the tribute paid to him in a remarkable book written by a Dutchman, Robert Sigmund – *Off at Last*, signifying the long spell of training and standing by waiting for their turn to come. Jimmy's 7th Battalion reunions in Dumfries for forty-three years have been hugely enjoyed by those airborne warriors. Mind you, they were not for the faint-hearted. You had to be in your place at H-5 (the designated hour for an operation to start) – or else. Morag was made especially welcome.

The most ebullient rugby player I ever met was undoubtedly Charlie Drummond. Born in St Boswells, son of the local sadler, he proved to have precocious talent both at school and on the rugby field for Melrose and Galashiels. While still at school he was playing for the Melrose 1st XV. Like many postwar internationalists, he would have won many more caps – he only won eleven – but for the war. He was also dogged by injuries. A very hardrunning centre and a fierce tackler, he was invariably targeted by the opposition. One particular injury cost Scotland dear. Early on in the Calcutta Cup match at Twickenham in 1947 he broke his collarbone. There were no replacements in those days and we went down 24–5 in a match which we should have won easily. After all, we had beaten them 27–0 the year before at Murrayfield. After hanging up his boots, he became an outstanding administrator and was President of the SRU in its centenary year, 1973. It was his vision that led to the foundation of the SRU Centenary Fund, which helps players who have been severely incapacitated at rugby. It has now raised very considerable sums for this great charity. Charlie's stamina was fantastic. He and his great mucker Micky Steel-Bodger, the President of England and the Barbarians, would carouse the night away in the North British Hotel and never show the slightest sign of fatigue the next day. The Army made a mess of Charlie's wartime service in the KOSB. Promoted almost immediately to the rank of *Platoon* Sergeant Major, an unusual rank which only lasted a year or two, he was posted to Cairo, where he and brother Ben, old pals from the Greenyards, got up to some highjinks and frittered away the war in some desk job. A waste of talent. Today he would have been immediately commissioned and given a platoon of Jocks. His dear widow, Kathleen, said of him: 'Yes; he was a great man but he was *a beggar* to live with.'

Nobody usually has a good word for civil servants. One of the persons I admired most during my Army career was Philip

Moore (now Lord Moore of Wolvercote), then the Deputy High Commissioner for South East Asia in Singapore. We were old opponents from the rugby field – he, Oxford University and England, I, London Scottish, Army and Scotland. Mercifully, I had never served in the Ministry of Defence (and kept that up to the end – though I had a narrow squeak) and it was an eye-opener to me to see how the Foreign and Commonwealth Office ran their affairs. In the Services we were trained to keep our communications short. Not so in the FO; their despatches ran for pages and pages right down to details about the personal habits of individuals who were causing disruption of the UK's plan to decolonise. With his charming No. 2, Alec Ward, we survived some fairly tense moments of international strain. It was no surprise that Moore later became Secretary to Her Majesty the Queen. The former Prime Minister of Singapore, the world-famous Lee Kuan Yew, would be the first to admit that the present superiority of Singapore and Malaysia owes a lot to the foundations provided by Philip Moore and the Earl of Selkirk and his staff.

Most people in the British Army affect to despise Her Majesty's Brigade of Guards. They reckon they are elitist, pampered, never subject to cuts like other regiments, and their officers are a lot of chinless wonders from Eton and Harrow who spend their time living it up in London town. *Nothing could be further from the truth*. The Brigade of Guards set the standards for the best Army in the world (at least it was). They play a full and distinguished part in Britain's operational commitments and, at the same time, are capable of performing ceremonial duties which are the pride of the nation and the envy of the world. They also provide key instructors for another of Britain's great success stories, the Royal Military Academy at Sandhurst. Not only does the RMA turn out a succession of highly proficient Army officers, but it also accepts and trains a goodly number of potential officers and leaders of foreign countries. The world would be an even more dangerous place today were it not for the web of outstanding soldiers and leaders who have been trained at Camberley. I was privileged to have Regimental Sergeant Major 'Dusty' Smith, Coldstream Guards, as my RSM at one point in my career. I've never known a man gain so much respect from so many people. He was an example of the British Army at its best.

Praise for the Guards should not belittle in any way the competence and loyalty of the Infantry of the Line, the backbone of the British Army. Every officer could quote examples of men (and now women) from quite humble backgrounds who, after training and experience, become magnificent leaders. I was fortunate to have two such in my company in Malaya – Pat Devenney MM and Felix Harrison. It seemed almost a crime to put a young National Service officer, after four months' training at Eaton Hall, in charge of a Platoon with these two hardened veterans under him as Platoon Sergeant. But this is the system and it has worked well over the years. Pat won a sizeable sum of money in the lottery – it's good to know that some sensible people do win – and emigrated to Australia. I just wish Felix – or 'Harryraya' as we nicknamed him after a local religious festival – could have been with us in September 2005 when 320 members of 1st Battalion KOSB met in Peebles to celebrate fifty years since the end of the Emergency in Malaya. I had hoped that they would all be presented with the medal which Malaysia have generously struck to thank the troops and rubber planters who took the brunt of casualties. New Zealand and Australia accepted the medal graciously but the Brits – you guessed it – turned it down. The ways of the men in grey suits in Whitehall are weird and wonderful. Subsequently it was announced that the medal might be awarded – but could not be worn! What a fudge – what a fiasco. The Lady in the House of Lords representing Defence said that one of the reasons it was turned down was that it 'was a long time ago'. It may have been a long time ago for her but not for the veteran National Servicemen who came to the reunion, many of whom intend to return to Malaysia in October 2006. I hope to be there with them and I do so hope they will be wearing their medals.

The best soldier in the Scottish Division in my book was Colonel Clive Fairweather. His reputation is firmly based in his primary role as an outstanding officer in the KOSB, but he was also a key member of the SAS in Northern Ireland and in the siege of the Iranian Embassy – no matter how well you know him he won't divulge anything – uniquely two commands as a Lieutenant Colonel, Depot Glencorse and 1 KOSB, both hugely successful. He eventually carried out my old appointment of Divisional Brigadier of the Scottish Division, but by this time they had meanly downgraded the appointment to full Colonel. He then retired, only to be head-hunted by the Scottish Executive as Chief Inspector of Prisons in Scotland. It was quite clear from all the newspaper reports that he did an outstanding job. He gained the respect of all the Prison Governors and was firm and fair to the prisoners. His reports and recommendations were not well received by the 'high heidyins' of the Scottish Executive. It was clear to one and all that he was doing his job too well – and they unfairly sacked him after an outstanding five years. I have met Scottish Prisoner Governors who mourn his loss. I tried to get Clive to tell me some of his experiences with Jim Wallace, the Minister for Justice and the first minister he served as Chief Inspector of Prisons. His usual SAS discretion caused him to be reluctant. However, he did admit that the former Secretary of State for Scotland Mr Michael Forsyth spread it around that he was a 'pinko'. Later Clive certainly saved the bacon of his boss – now Lord Forsyth – when, during a radio programme, a prisoner from Barlinnie asked: 'Does the panel think that after Bertie Vogts's performance last week there should be 6,349 prisoners in Scottish jails, not 6,348?'

The noble Lord put his hand to his mouth and whispered to Clive: 'Who the f— is Bertie Vogts?' (He was of course the unsuccessful Scotland football manager.) As Clive's replacement, the Scottish Executive appointed – praise be! – an ex-Moderator of the Church of Scotland – a great loss to the Kirk.

In the Army, I always hated the words 'other ranks', meaning those of Warrant Officer rank and below. I was quite happy for the officers, commissioned by the Queen, to be 'set apart', but the expression I prefer is 'officers and soldiers'. There was someone I never served with in action, but I did serve with after the war, when he was Regimental Sergeant Major of the KOSB Depot at Berwick. I was a Captain – but I was terrified of him! The one and only 'Fister' Walls. (I suppose he had been a regimental boxer in his younger days.) He was the life and soul of every party in the Sergeants' Mess – but watch out for him the next morning! Spotlessly turned out, and ready to jump on any offender of any rank. That was 'Fister' in barracks, but in action in Normandy with 6th Battalion KOSB there was no spit and polish but a field soldier of the highest courage and bravery, carrying out the principal roles of the RSM in battle, both ensuring that discipline is kept at the sternest level and keeping the forward troops constantly supplied with ammunition, which he achieved at great danger to himself. He was awarded both the Military Cross, a decoration usually granted only to officers, and the Military Medal, a unique combination. On a lighter note, 'Fister' reminded me of that cartoon of the Guards Sergeant Major leaving the front door for his work, with his pace stick under his arm. His 'ever-loving' looks him up and down and says: 'Have a good day, dear – be grumpy!' In action, 'Fister'.

Servicemen are traditionally uninterested in politics, taking the view – a plague on all your parties, they never look after the Services properly until their mismanagement causes a war or they fear war to be looming. But we do have the vote and an opinion. Churchill, of course, was head and shoulders above the rest; Attlee did a good job at an extremely difficult time in our nation's history; Sir Alec Douglas-Home was proof that the job of Prime Minister could be held by a gentleman; and in that class I would also put Labour Prime Minister Jim Callaghan. I'm afraid the Lady Thatcher ruled herself out of this admiration society for having the utter impertinence and incompetence to impose the Poll Tax on Scotland as 'try-on' for the UK. No wonder we got devolution.

It always amazes me when I read the Honours List twice a year that those in the pictorial headlines are always from the world of entertainment. It's true that they play an important part in our lives. My selection will hardly be recognised by most readers of this chapter. From before the war Flanagan and Allen had us rolling in the aisles (you never hear 'Underneath the Arches' these days); in wartime the radio show *ITMA* (*It's That Man Again*) was a major factor in keeping up morale. After the war, there were at least two films or shows we could see over and over again: *The Sound of Music* and *My Fair Lady*. The Two Ronnies were unbeatable – how I loved Barker in *Porridge* and *Open All Hours*. When *Dad's Army* first came on television most soldiers and ex-servicemen were horrified, calling the BBC all sorts of names for taking the mickey out of the Army once again. Opinions changed pretty quickly and the cover on this book proves that there's one fan right here. I was mighty proud to meet them – a class act which has stood the test of time.

On radio, one has to admire John Humphrys, James Naughtie and the others who get out of their beds at 4.30 every morning to keep us up-to-date with the world.

In journalism, Sir William Deedes is out on his own and, in Scotland, Allan Massie keeps up a remarkable work rate both in *The Scotsman* and the *Sunday Times*. The *Sunday Post* is a world-beater; characters such as the Broons and Oor Wullie are surely eternal.

In music, I admire the Royal Scottish National Orchestra and have done since the age of eight and for about four hours every day I am buoyed up by Classic FM. Bagpipe music, well played, at any time.

I have admired many ministers of the Kirk, most of them Army Chaplains (see Chapter 6). One who was not an Army padre but would have made a very good one was the Reverend Charles Robertson of the Canongate. His predecessor, the Very Reverend Ronald Selby Wright, had been my wartime padre and I naturally followed his post-war career with great interest. His involvement with the Canongate Kirk was immense and it was a shock to the system to learn, when he retired, that Presbytery and '121' (the HQ of the Church of Scotland is located at 121 George Street in Edinburgh) were not to permit this ancient kirk to appoint another minister, arguing that the parish was well served by the nearby St Giles. The Canongate fought and won. They called a completely unknown minister, Charlie Robertson, who for twenty-eight years served the parish faithfully and well. During his time a whole series of improvements have transformed the lovely building into a historic shrine, and kirk to Her Majesty when at Holyrood; the structure has been made safe (with invaluable help from an old friend, Adam Lothian), and there is a magnificent new organ and a thriving congregation. Recently retired, he will be sadly missed.

I seek no honours, for I have had more than my fair share already, but I have to say that I am a huge admirer of our Royal Family. I read the Court Circular meticulously every day. I just wish that more people did. I am absolutely staggered by the number of engagements all the members of the Household carry out each day. I've been used to rushing about a bit in my life and working to a schedule set by someone else. By any standards the work-rate of 'the Royals' – I hate the expression but it is much in use – is phenomenal. Five, six, seven engagements in a day is nothing unusual – meeting many, many people and remembering many of their names, a feat of dedication and service which the people of Great Britain and the Commonwealth should strive to emulate. They set us a wonderful example.

If I had to set down the name of the person I have admired most during my Army and civilian life, I would nominate Colonel Donald Ogilvie Hogg, OBE MC TD JP DL, soldier and farmer, of Kersmain, Roxburgh. His decorations speak for themselves. He was not a regular KOSB but served continuously in the Territorial Army and cadets from 1934 until the age limit for retiral had to be obeyed. He had all the qualities one admires in a man – he was brave, he led by example, he had a wonderful sense of humour, he was a loving husband, father and grandfather, he was an elder of the Kirk and, in his day, he was a good piper. How could one not admire a man whose 'cuddy' was called . . . Galloping Gertie?

Whaur's ma sheep?

Chapter 12

A LIFE FULFILLED

Abhor that which is evil, cleave to that which is good,
Be kindly, affectioned one to another with brotherly love;
Not slothful in business; fervent in spirit; serving the
    Lord.
Rejoicing in hope; patient in tribulation; continuing
    constant in prayer.
Distributing to the necessity of saints; given to hospitality.
Bless them that persecute you; bless and curse not.
Rejoice with them that do rejoice; and weep with them
    that weep.
Be of the same mind one toward another. Mind not high
    things but condescend to men of low estate. Be not
    wise in your own counsel.
Recompense to no man evil for evil. Provide things
    honest in the sight of all men.
If it is possible within you, live peaceably with all men ...
If thine enemy be hungry feed him; if he thirst give him
    drink.
Overcome evil with good.

Romans 12: 9–21

I reckon that St Paul said it all! He certainly went through a lot of experiences before he wrote these classic words. You couldn't get a better definition of 'the good life' than that. I wonder if it was written before or after he was shipwrecked off Malta?

Comparing one's own life with these 'commandments'

leaves one a little awed to say the least of it. How could one human being live up to such saintly behaviour without becoming a boring introvert? But goals are set for men and women just the same as they are for fitba' players and we all, said he pontificating, try to live up to certain standards. It is the standards that are the trouble with the present world. Sad to say – and every 'auld yin' says this – the standards of society in the twentieth century sank lower and lower as each year went by.

As I am nearly knocking on the age of eighty-eight, I think the time has come to sum up – to look back at the 1900s, to say what was wrong and then look at the twenty-first century and try to envisage the world which our grandchildren will have to live in.

By any criterion the twentieth century was just awful. Realistically, it must surely be the worst ever, 'wot with' the atom bomb, two World Wars ridiculously close to each other, constant minor wars cropping up one after the other in southern Europe, the Middle East and Africa. And we've had so many natural disasters – culminating in this century's tsunami – that you begin to wonder if the story of Noah and the Ark must have been true. To reverse the title of that fine charity, Saints and Sinners, it certainly was a century memorable for its many Sinners and just a few Saints. The Sinners roll off the tongue – Kaiser Bill, Adolf Hitler, Benito Mussolini, Joseph Stalin, Hirohito, Idi Amin and Saddam Hussein. Don't worry Mr Mugabe; I think you'll make it in due course; in fact, there are many, many white farmers who made Rhodesia's success story, who would put you there right now. I hope one day you will feel ashamed, but I doubt it. It's a struggle to list the Saints – Mahatma Ghandi, Pope John Paul II, Nelson Mandela, the Dalai Lama, Her Majesty Queen Elizabeth II. I'm just about stuck there.

One's memories of each decade centre around certain

events which stick out in experiences of the time. Everyone will have different landmarks. My first was certainly the General Strike of 1926. I was eight years of age and not much interested in anything but rugby football, but I was sufficiently aware of the world situation to know that Great Britain was on the edge of a political abyss. The First World War wasn't very long over and there was considerable unrest in the country. Communism had spread among the demobilised, disaffected, unemployed troops standing in the benefits queue, known universally in Scotland as 'the burroo' (from the French *bureau*). I saw ex-servicemen in the gutters of Glasgow, bare-footed, selling boxes of matches. The Russian Revolution was still fairly fresh in adults' minds and the pot could easily have boiled over, certainly in Glasgow.

The Thirties were all preparation for war and then the phoney war – the months of 1939–40 between the declarations of war and the outbreak of hostilities. It was fascinating being in London (as a copper) and seeing the preparations at first hand, air raid shelters, anti-gas kit, wailing sirens for 'enemy aircraft approaching' and continuous siren for 'all clear' (and one lived long enough to experience it for real), seeing Chamberlain in the flesh returning from Munich with a scrap of paper in his hand, indicating 'peace in our time'. Political bluff, playing for time. 'They' say that the Second World War could have been prevented if we had re-armed in time. Not a hope. In the early 1930s, we were on our knees financially after the Wall Street crash and the consequent Depression. Nothing would have stopped Hitler making war. He had made up his mind in *Mein Kampf* – and we should have been more prepared. How on earth the 'nice' Germans were taken in at Munich and afterwards beggars belief. They were just as guilty as the Nazis. In another context the other night someone whispered to me: 'See what happens when a Corporal gets power.'

To have lived through 1939–45 and not seen active service

would have been unbearable for any spirited young man – and, by this time, woman too. This brings one back to the question of Britishness and devolution, the nation state and patriotism. Those who lived through 1940 and 1941 will remember the fantastic spirit which ran through the British Isles at that time. We were so convinced that we were to be invaded by a foreign power that everyone, man, woman and child, was prepared to die for their country. The younger generation will think me daft when I say that the Home Guard were issued with *pikes* when rifles or submachine guns were unavailable, but it was an ambience which I have not experienced since. We would all cheerfully have gone to the mountains and caves to fight to the last. And we meant it. The prospect of the British Isles and the Republic of Ireland under the Führer was too dreadful to contemplate – but it was Great Britain we were fighting for, not Scotland, although Scotland punched well above her weight.

Like the First World War, they said it would be over by Christmas, but it was to be a long war and a long wait for everyone. Once the perfidious Italians had joined their Germanic mates it soon blew up into a world conflict. For the sake of posterity I am glad that my own puny efforts are recorded in a book, *With the Jocks*, by one of my regimental colleagues in the KOSB, the late Peter White. At the end it was a revelation to live in Germany and watch that virile nation climb back into civilisation again. And later to serve in Berlin, surrounded by the Soviets, but administered fairly by four nations, Great Britain, the USA, France and Soviet Russia. Visiting the Russian war memorials in Berlin we were overawed by the domination of that huge country. As I write these words, Mr Putin announces 'a bomb to beat all bombs'– oh dear! Will we ever learn?

The 1950s and 1960s were centred, for the British Army, in the Middle East and Far East. The Emergency in Malaya was the first experience I had had of the power of Communism in the former colonial territories of Britain, Holland and France. Perhaps Chin Peng, the indomitable leader of the insurrection in Malaya 1945–58, should be listed among the Sinners. It took the loss of hundreds of British and Commonwealth lives to restore Malaysia under astute Tunku Abdul Rahman and Singapore under the ebullient Lee Kuan Yew. Singapore is now one of the most thriving and well-ordered (some say over-ordered) city-states in the world and Malaysia, spreading across the sea to Sabah, the Sultanate of Brunei and Sarawak, is now a stable democracy with huge tourist potential. Just before Azahari and his fellow Indonesians invaded Brunei, I had planned a nice holiday break from Jesselton, the old capital of Sabah, to take the family on the single-track railway to Sandakan (beat that for a romantic holiday location). Alas, it could only be in my dreams and I hope that it still flourishes. Fortunately, Mr Azahari was quickly dealt with by Major Ian Cameron MC, of the Queen's Own Cameron Highlanders, and several years of confrontation followed.

Before we leave the impressions of the twentieth century, with apologies and thanks to the makers of that delightful tea-towel entitled 'We are the Survivors', let all those of us born before 1940 recall that:

We were born before television, before penicillin, before polio shots, frozen foods, Xerox, contact lenses, videos and the pill. We were born before radar, credit cards, split atoms, laser beams, and ball-point pens, before dishwashers, tumble driers, electric blankets, air conditioners, drip-dry clothes . . . and before man walked on the moon. We were born before day care centres, group homes and disposable nappies. We never heard of FM radio, tape decks, artificial hearts, word processors or young men wearing earrings. For us 'time sharing' meant togetherness, a 'chip' was a piece of wood or a fried potato, 'hardware' meant nuts and bolts and 'software' wasn't a word.

Before 1940 'Made in Japan' meant junk, the term 'making

out' referred to how you did in your exams, 'stud' was something that fastened a collar to a shirt and 'going all the way' meant staying on a double-decker bus to the terminal. In our day, cigarette smoking was fashionable, 'grass' was mown, 'coke' was kept in the coalhouse, a 'joint' was a piece of meat you ate on Sunday to last for the rest of the week and 'pot' was something you cooked in. 'Rock music' was a fond mother's lullaby, 'Eldorado' was an ice cream. A 'gay person' was 'the life and soul of the party', while 'aids' just meant beauty treatment or help for someone in trouble.

We who were born before 1940 must be a hardy bunch when you think of the way in which the world has changed and the adjustments we have had to make. No wonder there is a generation gap today . . . but by the grace of God, WE HAVE SURVIVED!

We got married first then lived together (how quaint can you be?). We thought 'fast food' was what you ate in Lent, a Big Mac was an over-sized raincoat and 'crumpet' we had for tea. We existed before house-husbands, computer dating, and 'sheltered accommodation' was where you waited for a bus.

The second half of the twentieth century was dominated by the fall of the Soviet empire and the tearing-down brick by brick of the Berlin wall. The political map of Europe was beginning to change, aided and abetted by the vision of a European bond, in the view of some into a nation, of others a Union, but in mine a grouping of nation states, agreeing to trade openly together. Then came a new type of war – terrorism. The Brits were in it from the start with a fresh and continuing wave of terrorism and rioting in Northern Ireland, then it spread worldwide, most dramatically, in this century, to the United States and one of its allies, Israel. Wars broke out at random in the Balkans and the forces of the United Nations were constantly being committed by the Secretary General to restore the peace all over the world. There are not many encouraging signs. Afghanistan seems to hold a fascination for British politicians of every generation. The Russians tried and failed; now we are at it again.

Hey! You're not meant to be writing history – you're meant to be writing a *critique* – and a challenging one at that. What's wrong with the world? At every level, it lacks *discipline*, and by that I don't mean the left-right-left sort of discipline of the Forces but the moral courage to differentiate between right and wrong. That goes for nation states as well as the individuals within them. In the case of national politicians, they travel the world attending conferences which are meant to put the world to rights. After much debate – and expense – they make agreements, which are constantly broken. Kyoto, for example, stands out, whilst global warming continues unabated. United Nations Resolutions are regularly flouted – Israel being the prime defaulter in this respect – but it is a general malaise. The answer must lie with the United Nations; it is the only organisation we have to discipline the world, but it must be obeyed. Perhaps it's time that the Headquarters was moved from New York and into the centre of the Muslim world – with a strong 'out station' in China.

In our social lives discipline has seriously declined during the century. For a good part of the century young men and women lived their lives under military discipline when an order took the form, not 'Please will you do this', but 'You *will* do this or that'. (The Royal Navy say, 'You *are* to do it', which is, I suppose, a little more polite than 'will'.)

National Service in Britain from 1945 until 1962 undoubtedly turned out every two years another group of young people who knew how to dress properly, to deal respectfully with other people and with a knowledge of other parts of their own country and of the world which, above all, made them proud of their own 'neck of the woods', nation state and family. There are persistent cries for National Service to be brought back, even on a selective basis as in some countries. This is Cloud Cuckoo Land: A. We can't afford it; B. It would harm industry and commerce; C. I can't think of any political party which would propose it; and D. Most of all, the Services simply haven't got enough manpower to do their committed defence tasks without training batches of National Servicemen and Women. Who knows? Some politician may have the guts to propose it, and much good it would do the country, wars or no wars. And don't tell me it is 'militaristic'; the Swiss have slept with rifles in their bedroom cupboards for generations and never had to go to war. No wonder they get the vote for 'Best Small Country in the World', when Scotland – rather unfairly I feel – comes in last, apart from Austria. What have they done wrong? Apart from producing Adolf Hitler.

The gradual improvement in personal incomes has led inevitably to excess in many aspects of our private lives, nowhere more so than in the consumption of alcohol. No one would have believed in the first decade of the twentieth century that 100 years later young girls would go out together for the express purpose of getting drunk. Every Saturday night, in our major cities, and in the country too, drunken young men in gangs go looking for a fight, and this has led to the adoption by Parliament of ASBOs – Anti-Social Behaviour Orders. Our elders would never have needed to do that. The recipe then graduated from a clip on the ear, to breeks down and a thorough skelping with a slipper or cane, prison with or without hard labour, or, in the case of capital crime, the gallows or a medicinal alternative. Even to suggest that one approves of the death penalty leaves one open to abuse. But the Americans still believe in it, as the ultimate sanction, as do the Muslim countries.

An Edinburgh taxi driver told me the other night that he is seriously thinking of giving up work on a Saturday because he always comes across fighting in some part of the city. It's nearly always quasi-sectarian, between Hearts and Hibs supporters.

That weekend both clubs had won by 3–0 so why the need to fight? 'Man is vile.'

One of the customs of the mid-twentieth century which I have found difficult to assimilate is sex before marriage. I must say at once that I am not inexperienced in sexual affairs. Apart from a normal and happy marriage, as a London policeman I have arrested prostitutes in Vauxhall Bridge Road, for persistent soliciting; I have been in a Parisian brothel along with half of the Scottish Rugby XV, two of them playing the bagpipes; and I have experienced the sensation of a Japanese geisha girl run her hand up inside my kilt. All of this was considered 'sinful'. The custom was to fall in love with a girl, woo her, with probably passionate evenings just stopping short of 'going the whole way'. I'm not naïve – many gave way. Contraceptives were unreliable and the disgrace of 'putting a girl in the family way' was unthinkable. The penalty for those who slipped up and had to pay maintenance was paltry – 7s. 6d. a week – 37½ pence in new money. Many's the case I had to deal with concerning soldiers during the Second World War.

I suppose it was the advent of the miraculous 'pill' and even, for the careless, the 'morning after pill' which changed things. Couples, even at school, have sex apparently freely, although I suspect that a good deal of exaggeration and imagination goes on. Some lead to 'relationships', and there is a mad rush to buy a flat and live together. In many cases this has led in due course to happy marriages. In 2005–06 I have noticed a tendency for more engagements and marriages to be advertised in the national newspapers. For those that go wrong and split up? Well, perhaps that's the point of the whole thing. It's a trial; not every couple can guarantee to be sexually compatible and for that reason I think it makes sense, although I know it causes heartbreak in many a mother's breast. My generation looks back and says, 'We wiz robbed of ten years of jiggity-jig.'

Many other developments during my lifetime would have

appalled my parents, and I suppose the same sort of reaction affects every generation. People frequently quote the letter from a Roman – or was it a Greek? – complaining about the appalling behaviour of their young people before the birth of Christ. Homosexuality has been 'under cover' since the beginning of time and, for my part, I just wish it had stayed there, but no, the present generation want everything to be 'transparent'. Now we have authorised single-sex marriages and no doubt the law will soon permit them to adopt children. I can't think what it would be like to be brought up by two daddies or two mummies.

Euthanasia is another tricky one. I remember how shocked my parents were when two very highly intelligent friends of theirs, New Yorkers, at a fairly comfortable age decided to put their heads in the gas oven together. The Dutch, whom I respect very much, have decided to legalise it. I just hope it doesn't take on here. I feel desperately sorry for people in agonising pain and for those who have to care for them but I am confident that our doctors and senior nurses know how to deal with these cases circumspectly.

Many of our most brilliant inventions – fast cars, the television, computers, email, mobile phones – have led to a speeding up of life's routine, which has led to *stress* being the most common ailment in every age group, so much so that many people have taken to working at home, and that can be very effective, giving more time for relaxation, fitness and the family. I don't approve; life is about *people*. Institutions like schools, banks, lawyers' offices and so on must always remain to deal 'face to face'. The pressure of bureaucracy and piles of paper seems to get worse, despite all these technologies. Long gone are the days when the morning post consisted of letters from friends; now it's just a collection of junk put out by hopeful salesmen and, sadly, charity after charity.

The daily papers make very depressing reading. I suppose it

was ever thus, but the radio news, particularly in Scotland, seems to be dominated totally by murders and fitba'. Radio on the whole is bearable but television after its early promise has become extremely boring with hardly a programme worth watching. It is unbeatable for world events and for sport but there are very few programmes with any *gravitas*. Old favourites, involving people, like *The Antiques Roadshow*, are good value for the licence but there are precious few of them. The so-called sitcoms are dreadful; I simply cannot understand how people can give up the time to watch them. It is rather shameful for the BBC and ITV to have to admit that repeats like *Dad's Army* gain a bigger audience than shows which have been expensively produced. Newspapers on the whole are very much better value. We are fortunate in Britain to have such a huge choice stretching over every possible political creed. I still prefer the broadsheet papers – a format that is fast disappearing – rather than the tabloids, which tend to collapse the minute you open them up. Gone are the days when the advertisements and notices appeared on the front page! I think I preferred that to the glaring headlines which are intended to shock and often are grossly exaggerated. The obituaries in the high-quality papers still maintain a very high standard and the coverage of sport is excellent. My complaint in Scotland is that the principal papers ape the London papers and concentrate on national and international news, whereas it would be interesting to hear news of other parts of Scotland. The answer one gets is: 'Scotland has the best local papers in the world; it's all there.' That is all very well but one can't buy them all. I buy one, but it is very localised.

Some things in Scotland will of course go on for ever, such as *Oor Wullie* and *The Broons*. How could we exist without them? The nation owes a debt of gratitude to D. C. Thomson in Dundee for many things. The *Scots Magazine* too is a world-beater.

So much for the woes of the past. What about the future? What about the twenty-first century which our grandchildren will have to face? I have already said that the twentieth century was awful. I'm afraid I have to say that it is my fear that the twenty-first century may be even worse, possibly not for the same reasons. There will be wars for sure, but not the same kind of long-drawn out horrors of 1914–18 and 1939–45. The nuclear threat will always be there and unless man goes completely bonkers, which is always on the cards of course, everything will be done to stop a madman (or woman) pressing the button. Human nature doesn't change. I say again 'Man is vile' (too polite to say 'and woman'), and all the evidence of history tells us that crises will take place. The main cause is nearly always jealousy. In the playground we always favoured the other chap's 'jammy piece' rather than our own – and so it goes for nations. We've seen it over and over again. There will be small wars and governments will find it more and more difficult to find troops who are prepared to risk their lives in someone else's cause. There was the recent case of the United Nations trying to raise a fairly large force to return to Afghanistan, but one member of NATO said it was 'too dangerous' and their troops would need protection. I ask you: what are troops for?

Somehow or other the United Nations must be given more 'teeth' to deal with the inevitable frictions which will increase in the twenty-first century as the 'old order changeth' and nations other than the Big Nine will want to have their say in world affairs.

But it is not wars that present the biggest threat to the lifestyle of our grandchildren. The greatest threats are quite different and I list them:

The environment – global warming
Oil

Water
The economy – Asian takeover
The Pax Americana
The dominance of Islam

It is quite common to hear people say: 'All this talk about global warming is just trying to frighten us.' Sorry – 100 per cent wrong. The evidence is building up all the time. 'When I was a boy' (here we go again) we skated on Tannoch Loch in Milngavie every year without fail. There was always one day in the year when the Academy Rector had to admit that skating fever would be a severe interruption to lessons and he declared, after 'Prayers', a Skating Holiday, to tumultuous cheers. The Scottish Bonspiel, requiring at least seven to nine inches of ice was held every year at Carsebreck Loch near Greenloaning in Perthshire. Passing in the train afterwards you could hardly see the shore for whisky bottles! The most recent bonspiel was held in 1989 at Scotland's only lake, the Lake of Menteith, near Aberfoyle. It was a huge success but there hasn't been one since, nor was there sufficient frost even in the Highlands to hope that it could be held. Before global warming, every village had its curling rink. Someone from Kelso told me the other day – and he's a good deal younger than me – that they reckoned to curl regularly outdoors until the middle of March. One year the thaw came so suddenly that the break-up of the ice from the rink, about a foot or more thick, actually threatened the old Kelso bridge.

There's no question we're warming up, but it's not all to do with temperature. The pattern of weather throughout the world is changing quite rapidly. The tsunami is the best evidence of that, but, nearer home, there is no doubt whatsoever that England has had two summers running which were much more inclement than Scotland, which was bathed in weeks of sunshine, apart from Argyll and the Western Isles, which exist perpetually under rain clouds.

We really must listen to the scientists, even though the 'expert', Professor James Lovelock, who developed the Gaia principle, is so gloomy as to be barely credible. He believes that the climate in which we presently live will only last for a limited number of years, and global warming will gradually increase the temperature worldwide, turning many parts of the world into unsustainable desert, until finally at the end of the century in 2100 the only place that normal life will be sustainable will be in the Arctic. Whew! 'Fasten your seatbelts.'

Undoubtedly, counter-measures will tighten up. Already, President Bush has told the gas-guzzlers of the USA to save gasoline. Of course, there's not the slightest chance of their taking any notice. Who is going to be the saviour? Once again, it can only be the United Nations, but that requires authority and discipline, not readily evident in most nation states.

All the remaining problems facing the inhabitants of the world in the twenty-first century are inter-related – oil, water, the economy, the dominance of Islam and the Pax Americana. I think we can forget the Pax Americana. I fear they have over-stretched themselves and will be forced to retreat by a combination of those other factors.

Oil will dry up eventually and there will be the most almighty scramble to see who can hang on the longest. I would predict that, by the middle of the twenty-second century, people will take up riding again seriously and will take shares in the companies who can run the best inter-city service horse-drawn. Shipping will boom again; well, there may be some kind of fuel but sail could well come into its own once more.

It's the same with water. Already our hearts are regularly assailed by tear-jerking pictures of children in Africa, who may depend only on muddy water carried for miles on their mothers' backs. It's not going to get better, no matter how hard the charities try. There will have to be a redistribution of water worldwide. We could start in Scotland. Already, the south of England is short of water every year whereas parts of Scotland, like Argyll, pour millions of gallons daily into the sea. If we can take oil by pipeline from Buchan to Grangemouth, why on earth can't we take water by pipeline from Argyll – at a cost! – to the shrivelled reservoirs in the south of England? Israel is already using water as a political weapon. They depend entirely on the snows which normally fall regularly on Mount Hermon. When they melt they top up the Sea of Galilee, which controls the amount of water that goes to Israel and how much goes to Palestine and the West Bank. Don't have any romantic illusions about the River Jordan. It is just a muddy trickle.

Maybe that's enough doom and gloom for now. There's one thing to bear in mind – the secret to a happy retirement is to find a home where your milk, papers and mail are delivered by nine o'clock every morning.

Oh, stop yer blethering, Frank!

Further Reading

Bibliography of the King's Own Scottish Borderers
There are over sixty books, booklets and articles relating to the history of the KOSB. Those of substance are as follows.

Early days
Captain R. T. Higgins, *Records of the King's Own Borderers or Old Edinburgh Regiment* (London, 1873)
Brigadier General M. G. Richardson and A. Ross (Glasgow, 1919)

Boer War
Lieutenant W. Home, *With the Border Volunteers in Pretoria* (Hawick, 1901)

First World War
Captain Stair Gillon, *The KOSB in the Great War* (London, 1930)

Second World War
Captain H. Gunning, *Borderers in Battle: The War Story of the KOSB 1939–1945* (Berwick-upon-Tweed, 1948)

There are also histories of the 4th, 5th, 6th and 7th Battalions. Richard Sigmond's history of the 7th Battalion, *Off at Last* (1997), is a remarkable work.

After the Second World War
Bob Woolcombe, *All the Blue Bonnets: The History of the King's Own Scottish Borderers* (London, 1980)

Korea
Major General J. F. M. McDonald, *The Borderers in Korea* (Berwick-upon-Tweed, 1952)

For further information, consult The KOSB Regimental Headquarters and Museum, Ravensdowne Barracks, Berwick-upon-Tweed, TD15 1DG; tel.: 01289 307426 or 307427; kosbmus@milnet.uk.net

Website
www.kosb.co.uk